STAINED
FORTUNE

JOE CALDERWOOD

Published by Water Street Press
Healdsburg, California

Cover art by thecovercollection.com
Interior design by Matt Schubbe

ISBN-13 978-1-62134-350-9

Get the Water Street Crime Starter Library FOR FREE

Sign up for the no-spam newsletter and get four full-length ebooks—the thrillers ***BLOODY PARADISE, FROM ICE TO ASHES, TROPICAL ICE***, and ***SING FOR THE DEAD***—plus two introductory short stories by the author of ***STAINED FORTUNE*** and lots more exclusive content, all for free.

Details can be found at the end of *STAINED FORTUNE*, or go here now:
https://mailchi.mp/waterstreetpressbooks/clintkennedy

This book is dedicated to my life partner of thirty-nine years and spouse of five, Gil, for all his support.

ACKNOWLEDGMENTS

I'd like to thank Grant Spradling who, twelve years ago while we lived in Merida, Mexico, encouraged me to write down my stories. I'd also like to thank Cynthia Drew who encouraged me to continue writing.

1

I HAD NOT PLANNED on ending up back in jail. But when the rewards are great, the risks are often greater.

I remembered how it felt the first time I'd entered jail, the edge of fear that seemed to jab at my nerve endings like the tip of a knife—a sensation I did not find completely unpleasant. Ambition had landed me here, certainly, but I couldn't discount that the nearly carnal satisfaction of an adrenaline rush didn't have something to do with how high I was willing to aim, or how far I'd go to meet my goals.

The other inmates—six in the cell of the Mexican jail I was led to—were hard-pressed to contain their desire to pounce on me as I took my seat among them on the cold, damp concrete floor. Child molesters, rapists, robbers, murderers, assorted minor scam artists—my new compatriots, their hair gelled to porcupine points at the top of their heads, dusty feet in battered flip-flops, dark and shining eyes assessing me.

The prison housed hundreds in cramped cells like this, dungeons with a toilet as the feature at the center of the room, a dank, brown liquid coagulated at its base and a metal seat for seven or more prisoners to use—no privacy and no toilet paper. Weeds sprouted from the cracks in the concrete floor, and the small, damp room smelled of body odor and spent bodily fluids. It was clear the toilet didn't get a lot of use; the inmates pissed wherever they stood.

Pedro, Luis, Gustavo, Manuel, Jose, Carlos—I was the only one with white skin among the mix of Spanish, Mayan, and Mexican prisoners. Most spoke Spanish, or Mayan, with only a spattering of English among them, but I spoke enough Spanish to make myself understood, and to understand that their conversation was about me, and irreverent.

Fortunately for me, Mexico—unlike America in these early years of the new century—was still an aspirational country. My new prison friends appreciated American men like me: they didn't resent my fresh, new, costly clothes or my expensive haircut;

2

they enjoyed the appearance of money, and their proximity to someone who looked like he had a lot of it.

2

THE INTENT TO make my fortune was what had landed me in jail the first time, but make my fortune I had, in spite of the temporary obstacle of incarceration. At just thirty-four, and with a fat bank account, I'd moved to Mérida, in the Yucatan, "The White City" named for the common color of its old buildings, and for its cleanliness. I'd bought and restored an eight-bedroom colonial mansion for my home. I spent my days drinking beer by my pool, reading a book or watching an old movie on TV, and feasting on the local dishes my houseboy, Pedro, prepared for me—*Poc Chuc* and *Papadzules*. My nights were spent drinking Scotch and making the rounds of restaurants, art galleries and the symphony that made up the vibrant cultural life of the city. The Mérida population includes the largest percentile of indigenous persons in Mexico—Mayans, most of whom were still struggling to reach even the lowest rung of the ladder their Mexican neighbors sat upon—and so I took it into my head that I would help them in their rise, though perhaps in an even more practical way than I'd been helped in mine: I'd bought three additional old colonials, each smaller than my residence, though just a few streets away, and was in the process of combining them into one building and restoring it as a school for Mayan kids. It was a deeply and not surprisingly satisfying way to spend my time, and my money.

Taavi, for one, wouldn't have been surprised. Maybe he was the one who put the idea in my head in the first place—roused himself from eternal sleep and whispered it to me in my dreams. That would have been something he would have done, if at all possible, and who was to say it wasn't?

In any case, my life was paradise, and it wasn't enough.

Who's to say what's "enough"? What is plenty for one man is paltry to another. I had wads of dollars in my pocket and stacks in my safe and rows and rows of numbers on my balance sheets, but when it came to thrills, I was poverty-stricken.

About three months after my move to Mexico, in the early spring of 2008, I volunteered as a worker for the Yucatan elections—the one hundred and six "municipal presidents", or mayors as we call them in the U.S., that were to be elected that May. Those few weeks of volunteer work consisted mostly of answering phones in various campaign headquarters, posting yard signs where they were permitted—and sometimes where they were not permitted, approaching area business people with a fundraising pitch on behalf of the resident power brokers and decision makers. You could call me a "people person". From the time I was a kid, I could always pick out the ones who would be most beneficial to know. I worked my ass off for the local pols and, by the time the elections were over, I had a whole new group of friends. Politics is an inherently dirty business and the pollution among the Mexican political class is deservedly legendary; I figured someone in that crowd could get me into a little bit of much-needed trouble.

My trouble came with a name: Alvaro.

I met Alvaro—met him *formally*—at the victory party for the candidate in Mérida's Third District. He—Alvaro, not the candidate; the candidate was a forgettable little puke who would later be indicted for removing his opponent's advertising materials and exchanging cash for voting cards—was a solid six feet tall, with a body of lean muscle

7

and a head of wavy, thick black hair. Even at first glance he seemed too lithe and graceful—too *physical*—to be a politician. Periodically he'd throw an arm around the smaller but exceptionally beautiful man at his side; the way he looked down at his companion, the smile he gave him, made me wonder if they were a couple. Both of them were surrounded by the circle of spectators who'd gathered around Alvaro, a crowd of men and women who looked up at Alvaro less as just another guest at the victory party but as if they were his fans. There were a few people among that crowd who looked too alert and wary to be simply guests; they looked like Secret Service guys if Secret Service guys routinely dressed in Irish linen guayaberas.

"Do you know who that is?"

"What?" I turned to the Mayan who'd been on the candidate's PR team. I didn't catch his name, but he looked enough like Taavi to draw me to him when I'd first arrived at the party and he'd taken it upon himself to give me the lay of the land—point out the important people I might like to know.

He gestured now toward Alvaro with the hand that held his frothy cocktail. "You think you recognize him, don't you? He's Alvaro Moreno, the bullfighter—not as well-known as his brother, Oscar, but Alvaro's the one who stabbed and killed the Intimidator."

I nodded. "I've never been to a bullfight in my life."

3

"**P**OLITICIANS AND BULLFIGHTERS, there is no difference between them," Alvaro told the crowd. "If you are a bullfighter, the bull is your opponent. He is the one you are trying to beat in the race, the one you do not want to lose the election to, hmmm?" he continued, and the people around him chuckled. "And everything a bullfighter does, every move he makes, is to do one of three things— distract his opponent, so the opponent is confused and can't fight back as well; anger his opponent, so the opponent makes a stupid mistake; cause injury to his opponent, so the spectators will see the bullfighter is strong and his opponent, this massive animal, is weak." By the time he finished, the people around him were laughing in earnest. He didn't need to twist to one side as if to dodge attack, his hands holding an imaginary cape, to keep his audience captive; that flourish at the end was all showmanship.

But when he'd twisted he'd ended up directly in front of me.

I stretched my hand out to him. "I'm Clint Kennedy. New to the area—"

Alvaro put up a hand and let his black eyes wander over my white skin, blonde hair, blue eyes. "New to the area? Who would have guessed such a thing?" he asked, sending the people who were still gathered around him into another gale of laughter.

I might have been put off—distracted—by his greeting, but that was just what he wanted.

"I've never been to a bullfight. I'd love to see you in the ring."

"You would?" he laughed, and he grabbed the beautiful man who'd been standing near to him and kissed him on the neck. "Then what do you say, Javier? I fight again in, what is it? Two weeks? Should we invite this Mister Clint Kennedy to be our guest?"

Javier shrugged, but he smiled as well. "I think Mister Clint Kennedy would like that, Alvaro."

"Then that's what we will do!" Alvaro boomed. He reached out at last to take the hand I had offered him. "Pleased to meet you, Clint. Call me Alvaro—and this is Javier, my brother-in-law."

Brother-in-law, I thought as I began to loosen my hand from Alvaro's grip in order to shake hands with Javier. *This relationship might be more complicated than I assumed...*

But I didn't get to either finish the thought or offer Javier my hand. Alvaro kept his fist tight over mine and yanked me toward him to whisper in my ear, "I know who you are, Mister Clint Kennedy."

4

"**Y**OU WERE ARRESTED for running an illegal business in Miami, Mister Clint Kennedy." Alvaro smiled but there was no humor behind the black eyes, the set of his mouth— not until Alvaro decided to put it there; it was a bit of magic I didn't miss, the way his smile broadened to show rather large but bright white, perfectly aligned teeth, and how he willfully allowed merriment to replace the glare in his eyes. "I admired how you fought the charges and, in the end, escaped with just a small fine."

It wasn't a small fine. Not to me. Not at the time. It was a big chunk of the money I'd set aside to create a new life for myself in Mexico, with Taavi. I had plenty, as I've said, but I couldn't let go of the idea that I could make the money back that I'd had to fork over for that fine—a gambler's curse, I suppose: the inability to stop playing when you've lost a hand, even if, overall, you're still a big winner.

The illegal business I'd run in Miami had been an escort service. Alvaro had been one of my top clients, though I'd never actually met him in Florida—and never knew his real name until I ran into him in Merida. I knew him only through the young men who worked for me—glimpses of him at a club with one of my employees, the giddy reports the next day from one of my boys or another about their tall, handsome customer: he liked to party; he was gentle in bed; he apparently had un-limited funds and wasn't shy about throwing around American dollars or spending them on his evening's date.

When I'd spotted him one afternoon at my gym in Mexico I'd asked Memo, my trainer, who he was. Memo had laughed. "Alvaro Moreno, one of our more famous sons, for bullfighting. That he's also a big-time drug dealer, well, that he keeps more under-the-radar." Memo had shrugged at the surprise in my eyes. "Public knowledge, unacknowledged—he's a big do-nor to the local politicians. Not one of them is going to say out loud where his campaign funds come from—the funds go away if the funder goes to jail, you know?"

I'd nodded and handed Memo a fifty-dol-lar tip.

Alvaro was still gripping my wrist. "What I don't know, Clint Kennedy, is who you paid off to get away with such a small fine."

I made myself smile back at him. "Paying people off is how business is done. I'm happy to compensate someone if it gets me what I want."

This made Alvaro laugh, and he let go of my arm if only to clap me, hard, on the back. "You are a smart guy, Clint Kennedy. Maybe, I'm thinking, we can do some business together. Are you interested?"

I nodded, the poker face I turned to him not wholly an act, merely the way business is done: never let a potential partner know how eager you are to get into bed with him.

The crowd around us, hundreds of people who, before Alvaro had singled me out, had been clamoring to be a part of the circle around him, became suddenly rowdy, as if the deference they had politely afforded an important man who seemed to want to have a private conversation was now expired. The attention of the crowd, I noticed, however, was focused on the doors to the banquet room and the newly re-elected officials who were starting to arrive to make their victory speeches.

"It's getting a little noisy in here. Why don't we go across the street to the café and have a drink?" He placed his hand on my shoulder without waiting for me to accept and started to guide me through the oncoming wave of humanity, toward the front door, nodding to his guys to follow. Javier elbowed ahead to open the door for us.

"Don't you want to speak with the municipal presidents, and—?" I offered as we walked, but Alvaro only grunted out a small laugh and squeezed my flesh in his big hand.

"Standing around waiting for a politician to shake your hand and nod at your request is for people who don't have the right telephone numbers in their cell phones."

I'd made a fortune running an illegal business. Been to jail for it. Come out on the other end with the fortune, and most of my pride, still intact. I hadn't felt as hopelessly naïve as I did that night under Alvaro's guiding hand since I'd been a teenager.

5

LET'S TALK ABOUT drugs—or, more precisely, why I had no moral hesitation about doing business with a Mexican drug dealer, because I didn't.

I've always been a free market kind of guy: let the laws of supply and demand set prices free from government regulation.

It's a good argument, as far as it goes—could form the core of the stump speech of any five politicians out of ten. But in a situation where the operative phrase is "supply and demand" and the demand is for drugs, all bets are off. It doesn't matter that if people didn't demand drugs, drug lords would be out of business fast enough—that they are merely servicing a broad market niche; the minute you mention drugs, you've grabbed hold of the third rail, swatted the sacred cow on the ass. Drugs harm people's health!

Drugs kill people! Drugs cause people to get into fights and act cranky and hang out with the wrong kinds of friends and go bankrupt and commit crimes and cause the downfall of civilization!

As if drugs were the only product on the market that weren't good for you, or drug lords were the only businessmen peddling goods with potential downsides. Profiting from someone else's misery. One in five kids in the United States is obese and on his way to a lifetime of diabetes and heart disease and nobody's trying to make an outlaw out of the hamburger-pushing clown. Thirty thousand people die in gun violence every year and the NRA's a goddamn religion to half the population. Almost five thousand families have buried a soldier who died in Iraq and Afghanistan since 2003—American families; almost five hundred thousand families in Iraq and Afghanistan have buried their war dead since then—but Halliburton is sitting pretty on almost forty billion in proceeds for that little enterprise and, so far as I know, Dick Cheney's still walking around a free man. I'm not complaining about that, just the hypocrisy burns my ass.

We were out on the sidewalk, waiting for traffic to open up so we could cross the street. Ancient, beat-up cars crawled both ways in front of us, releasing smoke and the occasional backfire. Drivers honked their horns, fireworks exploded overhead, a malnourished dog sped off at a particularly loud burst from above and three little dark-skinned kids ran after it, screaming in glee; the election was over and the party would be going on all night.

Alvaro's security detail walked ahead of us, stopping the cars with hand signals, thumping on hoods to get the attention of drivers more interested in the fireworks than pedestrians, making way for their boss, and for me.

The owner of the café met us at the door. "So nice to see you again, Señor Alvaro," he said, bowing ever so slightly. "My place is always available to you."

Alvaro thanked him with a wad of cash, a big smile and a tight hug, and we walked to the back corner of the café where his boys had pushed several tables together—one for Alvaro and Javier and me, and a couple in front of us where they could sit and keep an eye on the front door.

"I've got a big problem I think you can solve for me," Alvaro said as we took our seats, placing his hands on the table, right into a puddle of stale beer the waiter hadn't wiped away. He made a face and raised his hands for a napkin; Javier, three of the secu-

rity guys, and the owner all scurried as one
at his scowl.

I took the seat beside Alvaro. "Like I told
you before, I'm interested. You tell me what
it is, and I'll tell you if I can," I said, and then
waited while the rest of them attended to Alvaro's wet hands.

6

WE WEREN'T AT the café long, time enough to drink the tequila and eat the *chilaquiles* and *papadzules* Javier ordered for us. Alvaro teased out his proposition while we ate.

"The problem, Mister Clint Kennedy, is not a lack of money, but what to do with all of it I have," was as direct as Alvaro was willing to be at the table. I nodded in reply as if I completely understood his difficulty. What I didn't understand, of course, was how much money we were talking about. Fifty thousand is a lot of money to some people and I wasn't going to waste my time for peanuts.

Still, Alvaro had been on my radar since I'd spotted him enjoying the company of my boys in Miami and, clearly, I had been on his radar, too. It was discomfiting to realize how much he knew about me—that he'd done his research. I'd moved to Mexico for a

fresh start since I'd put my escort days behind me, but Alvaro put that old business
right in front of me again. My guess was that
my name had come up on a date with one
of my escorts. He probably knew my day
job back then had been as an agent at Merrill Lynch—for five years I'd built a book of
business, and for three years in a row had
been their top-grossing agent. I'd accepted
only those clients having a million or more
to invest.

On the other hand, the little dance he was
doing with me had an element of flattery—I'd
clearly been *chosen* and curiosity, if not ego,
demanded I find out for *what*. Alvaro was an
exceptionally attractive man, but I sincerely
hoped his purpose wasn't only to bed me,
though, if sex was part of a larger offer...
Well, I'd see. I'd made the decision nearly six
months before to enter into a period of celi-
bacy—you run an escort service and random
sex loses a big chunk of its appeal—but my
currently monkish lifestyle wasn't one I'd
ever considered permanent; and, anyway,
most business deals required the sacrifice
of some principle, large or small. My heart
was still battered over Taavi's loss, though I
was a realist; at some point I'd have to stop
mourning his death and get on with living a
life without him. Taavi, himself, would have
told me so. I'd bide my time to see what else

24

Alvaro was putting on the table. The food was exceptional and the tequila extra *anejo*, so I was patient.

When our plates were empty and our glasses were drained, Alvaro leaned back in his chair and wiped his mouth delicately with one of the stack of napkins that had been provided to him earlier in response to the spilled stale beer. He smiled at Javier, to his right, and clamped his left hand tightly onto my thigh under the table. His fingers were like a vise on that tender spot just above the knee, and I tried not to wince under his grip. "I think," he said, as if he had just made the decision, "it would be better to show you my predicament than to only tell you about it."

We rode in Alvaro's black, bullet-proof Hummer H2 SUT, the driver taking the three-lane Paseo de Montao at just over the speed limit, pressing on the pedal with less reserve as the road narrowed to two lanes out of central Mérida. Javier sat to Alvaro's right in the back cab, me to his left, the driver and a second factotum staring dead ahead at shotgun. Another vehicle followed us with the rest of Alvaro's men. I watched the headlights of the second car in the Hummer's rear-view mirror, silent in my awe at how the driver of that car kept a precise and consistent three car-lengths behind us no matter how the driver of the Hummer accelerated or slowed. The danger of driving through the night with a drug lord and his henchmen gave me the sort of buzz I hadn't felt in too long a time.

About ten miles outside of Mérida our driver turned right, onto a narrow, paved road, the driver behind taking the turn so smoothly right after him it might have been choreographed, and drove us another quarter mile to a fortress. We entered through a double-arched limestone gate, no doubt carved and erected sometime during the rule of Porfirio Diaz, in the late 19th or early 20th Century, when European architectural details had started to be fused with the older Spanish aesthetic, but the wrought-iron gates swung open seamlessly on electric power, and the guns the half-dozen guards inside the gate carried on their backs were the very latest in killing technology. The four men in the car behind us jumped out when their car had cleared the gate, but the Hummer's driver kept us moving deeper into the compound, the last hundred yards to the hacienda Alvaro called home.

The inner courtyard was a lush, tangled garden of royal palms, hanging pots of bougainvillea, and latticed ficus that must have taken some diligent gardener years to train. Beds and pots of calendula, gerbera, and impatiens were arranged by color. The walls surrounding us were painted pale yellow; the arches that punctuated them, and that led to the various living areas in the home, were bright white; the ground beneath us was paved with polished terra cotta tiles. All of this was illuminated with the soft, yellow glow from electric torches. Two of the interior living areas were lit more brightly and, though I couldn't see into them through the foliage, I could hear a television playing softly from one of them. Alvaro had his arm slung around Javier's shoulder as we entered but as we neared the center of the courtyard, I saw Alvaro squeeze him once and nod his head toward an arch on our left.

"Come this way," Javier said.

I thought for a moment he was directing me, but Alvaro's men, the driver and the somber shotgunner, peeled off with Javier toward one of the bright, interior rooms, and Alvaro's arm went around my neck. "You," Alvaro said, "come with me."

Our sandals made soft shuffling sounds on the tiles as we walked the rest of the way to the far wall of the courtyard, up three short terra cotta stairs, and under a darkened archway. Alvaro twisted the knob of one of the elaborately carved mahogany doors under the arch, and let go of my neck to find and flip a light switch. Even before the room was illuminated I could smell the musty odor of old paper money.

The room was large, maybe thirty feet by twenty, a guest room if you were to judge from the only piece of furniture in it, a sleigh bed—a pricey American antique, if I were guessing. But stacked floor-to-high-ceiling, on the bed and, assuming from the density of it, *under* the bed, were piles of money. American money, not new but soft and infused with the scent of commerce, sorted by face value—twenties, fifties, hundreds—and carefully packaged with rubber bands.

"The total is twenty million," Alvaro said. "Have you ever seen anything like it, my friend?"

I didn't reply immediately. I wanted a moment to take it all in. Then I said, "Yes." I had the urge to walk deeper into the room— as deep as I could, given that the piles were stacked nearly to the door—and put my hands on the cash. Touch it. Rifle the piles and get my hands dirty—but I had the distinct impression Alvaro's goons weren't ever far away and they would be in the room the second I made a move toward the loot. "Yes," I repeated, "I have. My best friend back in the U.S., his family owns a bank—a chain of banks, maybe eight of them now, maybe more. His dad used to take the two of us into the vault when we were kids, an object lesson in what could be ours if we worked hard—or, I guess, more of a lesson for *me*. Jack was always going to inherit the bank..." I was rambling—*twenty million dollars*—and stopped myself before spilling my whole history, one of four brothers raised by a hard-working, single mother, growing up poor but motivated, desperate to earn my keep—my place— in the world into which Jack and his father welcomed me... I wondered, suddenly, how much Alvaro knew about me. How far back his research on me went.

"That would be your friend Jack Cohen?" Alvaro asked. "Your friend whose father is the banker?"

I was shaken and impressed. "Yes, that would be Jack."

7

IT HAS BEEN widely reported that life goes on unmarked in only a few cities in Mexico—unmarked by the drug-inspired violence that disfigures large parts of the country. The leaders of the drug cartels are known as kingpins and, in 2008, the most feared cartel was the Zetas, though the might of the Sinaloans and the Gulf Cartel was nothing to sneeze at either back then. When two cartels were in competition? Then bodies by the dozens would be dumped to send a message—what is known as *narcomata*—which is, simply: "This is my territory. We are here and we are not leaving and you stay out." When territory was in dispute, the killings could become a daily ritual. The police were, in many cases, on the cartels' payrolls and those who weren't looked the other way in order to dodge any stray bullet that might have their name on it.

Circumstances changed in 2006, when Felipe Calderon was elected to the presidency. He declared war on the cartels. Calderon's then-two-year presidency had already cost over fifty thousand lives and left thousands more battered mentally and physically. My impression was that the populace was growing weary of his crusade and looking forward to the day they could vote him out in favor of someone who knew to leave the cartels alone. I knew Alvaro was connected with the cartels—he had to be because how else was an otherwise unemployed bullfighter going to end up with twenty million dollars in small bills in his spare bedroom?—and like a bored housewife itchy for juicy gossip, I longed to know more about the connection. Intellectually, I understood that the less I knew about his operation, the safer I would remain. But I also thought that if we went into business together, then someday Alvaro would let me in on the dirt. For now, what he wanted was his money out of his house.

Alvaro enjoyed protection from Mexican officials, from the police to the municipal president; he paid well for this pleasure. "I never have to go through immigration or customs when I travel back into the country," he told me, shrugging as if this were a small favor. "I love my country," he continued, adding an unnecessary, signature flourish with his arm, "but I don't love the banks here. The more money you have in a Mexican bank the more ways the government finds to take it away from you. You give and give and give freely to the politicians and still they make laws that rip your money from you by force. I think you feel the same way, Clint, because our bankers aren't enjoying much of your money either." He shrugged again when I blinked in surprise; I would have to get used to how very much he knew about my personal history—and finances.

"I want to move my money out of my country, and to do it quickly before so much more accumulates. My wife, you see, she has given me just this one room, and she begrudges me even this space—she wants another guest room, to make this room comfortable for when her parents come to visit..."

Wait. Wife?

Funny, the things you assume, the American-middle-class, hetero-centric perspective that can jam up the most astute gaydar: that Javier had become Alvaro's brother-in-law through the marriage of a sister or a brother. That Alvaro, himself, had a wife staggered me to the point that I actually had to reach out and hold onto the doorframe.

"I'll introduce you to her sometime. But what I want to know is can you get my money to the U.S. and into a bank there? If you can—and if you will—I'll give you twenty percent of it, right off the top. Do you think this is something you'd like to be involved with?"

Wait. Four million? Tax free? That would set me up for life. Of course it was something I'd like to be involved with. This was a conclusion I could reach before I even calculated the delicious risk of it.

I swallowed and looked at Alvaro—never show your hand, I reminded myself. "You know that some banks in the U.S. aren't completely stable right now? That some economists are predicting even more instability in the coming months—"

I watched him to see if he knew as much about my country's finances as he knew about my personal ones—or that Jack's family's bank was one of the more unstable institutions, currently undergoing an audit by FDIC. Alvaro waved my concern away as if it were an annoying insect, then threw an arm around my neck again and hugged me close. "You are a smart guy, Clint Kennedy. You will find a way to get my money up there to the United States and keep it safe. That's why I'm willing to give you such a generous cut of it!"

Of course he was right: he'd come to the right person. I knew the Feds were buzzing around Jack and his father only because his big, stupid brother Abe had made so very many questionable loans, most of which were never going to be paid back, and many of which were, even now, in default. Show the Feds there was enough cash on hand to keep the bank from imploding and they'd happily back off. This was, at least, the consensus Jack and his parents, David and Candace Cohen, had come to back in the early spring of 2008—the working premise he'd told me about in so many of the stoned, long-distance phone conversations we had late into the nights, the guiding principle he and his father were moved to act upon on two fronts: increase customer deposits and cultivate new sources of investor interest. Perhaps Alvaro had just handed me a way to help Jack attack on both fronts.

The one major problem I foresaw as I stood in that room, in the midst of all that rubber-banded cash, was how to get Alvaro's money into the bank without making its source obvious. The Feds would ask minimal questions about a cash infusion, but if there was a hint that one of the answers might be that it was drug money, well... As I've already said, drugs were the third rail; some sniveling, little government accountant would get his panties in a twist and make a stink that his other, more reasonable counterparts would be unable to ignore. Even to this thorny question, however, I thought I might have a solution—a way around bank security that had entered my mind one late, celibate night after Pedro had served me one too many beers as I lounged around my pool. The next day, stone sober, I'd fleshed out my theory and, now, it seemed I maybe had a reason to give it a real-world test.

"I'll need to talk with Jack," I said, "before I can give you an answer."

I also needed to do my own research— my own background check on Alvaro. I needed to make sure I wasn't being set up, the next big, splashy drug bust, a sting operation that was only for show—a show put on by the U.S. and Mexican governments to demonstrate for the press that they were serious about ending the drug trafficking business so all the real kingpins could continue about their business unmolested.

Alvaro smiled. He released his hold on my neck and clapped me, hard, on the back. "You are a careful man, Clint Kennedy." He laughed and flicked off the light in the guest bedroom so we were once again in the glow of the courtyard's relative darkness.

"If you need to travel to Florida," Alvaro told me as he closed the door to the room, "you can take my jet." He laughed again— what sounded more like a grunt—"I could even go with you! We could have a night on the town—Miami is such a good place for getting laid!" He made another grunt and, his mouth turned as if in mirth, adjusted his crotch and threw me a stare.

My immediate thought was, *Great, the offer does include sex.* Then I reminded myself that one of the things I'd noticed shortly after taking up residence in Mexico was that the men seemed to punctuate nearly every conversation by grabbing their crotches and adjusting their junk. It seemed to be a local custom in the way that Texans eat barbeque or Alaskans wear wool socks.

Still, if Alvaro's crotch-grabbing wasn't merely habit, well, four million dollars—tax-free—was good pay for a blow job. The idea of such a quick success, so much money, was making my mouth water in any case— and for four million dollars I'd have sex with man, woman or animal, though I might prefer not to. But when I turned to follow Alvaro down the three short steps back into the courtyard, I saw that he had stopped short, confronted with two small, beautiful boys. They were maybe ages three and five, both plump and black-eyed, dressed in linen shorts and thin, expensive cotton T-shirts, the older one holding a soccer ball.

"Ha ha!" Alvaro bellowed, genuinely laughing now, bending to scoop up the boys, one in each arm. "My sons, Clint, meet my sons! Alvaro Junior"—he bounced the older boy on his elbow—"and Javi"—he kissed the younger one so hard on the side of his head the boy shrieked with laughter. "I missed you boys today. Tell me, have you been good boys? Did you do what your mama told you to do, all day long? Tell me? Have you been good today to make me proud?"

The boys squirmed in his arms, under his kisses, laughing and shouting, "Yes! Yes! Play ball with us now, Papa, please, can you play now?"

Then Alvaro turned back to me. "You and I are going to play together soon, Clint! Don't forget!"

I nodded, noncommittally, though I doubt he noticed my level of enthusiasm didn't match his. "Let's see how business goes," I called back to him. "I need to go make some phone calls—"

"Sure, sure." Alvaro plopped his sons on the terra cotta and accepted the soccer ball Alvaro Junior handed up to him. "My driver will take you home, yes? Yes! Javier!" he shouted into the night. "Mister Clint Kennedy needs to go home. Come out here now; Clint needs a ride back to his house!"

A driver—a different one than had driven us to Alvaro's compound—and the same sullen shotgunner escorted me back to my home. I jumped out of the Hummer at my front door, waving the car away before I yanked my phone out of my pocket and dialed. I walked through the kitchen while it rang, indicating to Pedro, who was in there busily polishing the few pieces of silver service I had so far accumulated—candleholders that he had taken it upon himself to keep glowing pristinely, that I wanted a beer. I made my way out to my pool, chucking my shirt, and took a deep pull on the Bohemia Dark before my call was answered.

"I need to know everything you can find out about a Mister Alvaro Moreno," I said as soon as my party picked up.

8

"**A**LVARO MORENO WAS about nine years old when his father, also Alvaro—now deceased, so our Alvaro has inherited the title of Senior—enticed him and his younger brother, Oscar, to watch and learn bullfighting. The father was a well-known fighter in Mexico as well as in Spain—this was not so long ago, but well before bullfighting became so controversial. You know, I'm kind of surprised someone Alvaro's age is a bullfighter, considering how young people are mostly the ones who think of the sport as a cruelty from a past era..."

I shrugged. "It's a tradition down here. Traditions don't die out as fast as you think they do."

"Huh"—I couldn't tell if this was a grunt of agreement or not—"anyway, the father didn't let the sons start training for the ring until Alvaro was thirteen, so Oscar must have been, what, eleven? Yeah, that seems right. When young men start training for the ring they use young bulls who don't have their horns yet. There's a story, probably apocryphal, that young Alvaro wanted to kill his bull the first time he was in the training ring…"

"I just met the man and it doesn't sound untrue to me…"

"…and his coach had to stop him—they don't kill the bulls until they get older and become aggressive. But here's a story I think is true too: when Alvaro was fourteen he and the family's thirty-year-old housekeeper started a six-month affair—a liaison arranged by his father. A boy's gotta lose his virginity at some point, right? Might as well be with an amenable older woman, and this housekeeper was supposed to have been gorgeous…"

"A-huh."

"After six months, though, the father sent the housekeeper packing. Apparently with a nice cash payoff…"

"Why doesn't that surprise me?"

"You should see the photos of the teen-age Alvaro I found—check your phone; I just sent a couple to you—fucking hot, hot, *hot*! Like one of those early Spanish settlers you see in history books—dark and sleek, you know. I'd have tapped that."

"Focus on the business, for chrissake—"

"His debut fight was in the Plaza Del Torres, when he was eighteen. The stadium was full—twenty thousand people! It isn't usual for a newcomer to face such a large crowd, but his father was scheduled to fight later in the day, and, in any case, the fans wanted to see what the son of such a famous fighter could do."

"And? What could he do?"

"He killed it. I mean, figuratively and literally—fifteen minutes into the fight the bull hits Alvaro, knocks him over and the crowd goes wild, thinks the kid's been injured, but the kid gets up and, when the bull returns, turns and drives his sword right into his head. Listen, I found a newspaper account, 'I did only what my trainer instructed me to do: let the bull seem to have the upper hand and, then, when the bull thinks you are losing, you make your move for the kill'... Modest man, right?"

"Don't believe it."

"Don't worry. I don't. So, the only snag, it seems, for gorgeous young Alvaro was that Oscar was the better bullfighter. Had more of the father's natural abilities, at least according to the accounts I've been able to find online. Alvaro's not a bad fighter, nothing I've found says that, just that his brother's the one who got famous. Alvaro still has plenty of fans, but he only fights in exhibitions for the tourists, mostly off-season, like the one he invited you to in a week or so."

"And?"

"And when he stopped really fighting he started some businesses, all legit, used his father's fame, and his brother's, for entrée, and his father's associates were all too happy to back him financially..."

"All the businesses were legit?"

"*Are* legit. On paper, anyway. Construction material supply, a chain of pool cleaning services. What isn't on paper is that he's one of two local distributors for the Abeyta Cartel in Mérida..."

"Aha..."

"I guess his business partners figured anyone who would get in a ring with a killer bull can certainly deal with an incompetent government *and* the drug people..."

"So, he's clean."

"Clean."

"And you're in?"

"Why don't you come up to Miami and meet with Dad and me tomorrow?"

"Consider me on my way, Jack." I hung up the phone and chugged the rest of the beer Pedro had brought to me before I dropped my pants and dove into the pool. The potential of suddenly acquiring great wealth is enough to make anyone light-headed; I thought a dozen laps in the cool water might be enough to clear mine.

9

I FLEW OUT BEFORE dawn the next morning on Alvaro's Gulfstream G450, bound for Miami to meet with Jack and his father and proffer a business deal. How that deal would be structured was, at this point, anyone's guess—including mine.

Tim, Alvaro's handsome young steward, stowed my duffle bag—I planned on a short trip so I wasn't going to need a whole lot of changes of clothes—and asked me what he could bring me from the galley. "Coffee? Orange juice? A little bit of bubbly in the OJ, maybe, start the day off with a bang, not a whimper?"

"Thanks, Tim. Just coffee."

"Very good, Mister Kennedy." He turned to leave, then looked back, twisting his head only so I still had a full view of his backside as he walked away. "How do you take it?"

"Just black, Tim." I smiled and settled back on the sofa in the main cabin. "Just black."

If I'd boarded this jet without any idea of whose it might be, I realized, I would know it was Alvaro's. Two swooping sofas, covered in white leather, ran the length of the main cabin, strewn with plump pillows in gold and turquoise lamé. An oval table of high-gloss gold and white wood sat between them, along with a coffee table that rose to dining level—I discovered when Tim returned with my tray of coffee—with one light step on a pedal to activate the hydraulics. An arch of etched and frosted glass depicting a bull in full fury on one side and a matador swirling a furious cape on the other, defined the cabin's entry and, underfoot, there was a white carpet that walked a fine line between deep shag and shaggy fur.

I sat back on a surprisingly comfortable turquoise pillow and sipped my coffee—a dark roast with a hint of anise and absolutely delicious—and thought about how I could get Alvaro's money into Jack's family's bank. And how I could convince Jack and his father that it was in their best interests to help me do it. I knew their bank was, like many banks in that late spring of 2008, in deep trouble. Their particular trouble stemmed, as I've already indicated, from one of the era's common sources of problems: bad loans that had been made without appropriate collateralization and/or with outright falsified income statements, in this case by Jack's odious older brother, Abe. You wanted a half-a-million-dollar house but your combined family income was $35,00 a year? Abe would just add a '1' in front of that '3' on your application and no one, not his father or his brother or any of the other officers who were in on his scam could convince him that it didn't matter how much money the bank was in line to make because they had extended the loan; if—*when*—the homeowner defaulted because he couldn't afford the damned house the bank was going to *lose*. Jack and his dad had been scrambling for months to increase their capital so the Feds wouldn't take them over.

The beauty of dealing with Jack and his dad was that I could tell them the truth— they were, in many ways, my family, too. These were people who believed in me, cared for me extravagantly, and who would go— *had already gone*—out on a limb for my sake. Also, bringing Alvaro's deal to them offered a solution to their own problems. The ugly part was Abe. Abe and I had always been on opposite ends of friendship. I took comfort from Jack's final words to me on our phone call the night before: *I will do anything to save the bank.* I repeated his words to myself, took another sip of my excellent coffee, and settled in to contemplate my theory on how to breach bank security—how I could make this money transfer work.

10

ALVARO'S JET SETTLED down gently at Homestead Airport just as the sun was rising. As we taxied to the hanger I saw Jack get out of his silver Porsche 718 and flip his cigarette to the grass. He waved at the plane, assuming I was looking out the window at him, and started jogging over to the tarmac—an activity for which he was well suited as he was still in the bike shorts, tank top, and workout shoes he'd worn to spin class that morning.

"Now I call that style, my friend! What a hot fucking ride," he shouted up to me as the stairs came down.

"I'll show you the inside later," I called back, heading down the stairs to him, my duffle hoisted over my shoulder. "Focus on business first, Jack."

Jack had been my best friend since we were children, students in the same private school classroom, he a legacy student—his father and grandfather were both alumni, and his sadistic older brother was a couple of grades ahead of us—and me, there on his dad's dime, too, paid for partially, I am still sure, because his dad saw how close Jack and I were. I'd always tagged along with my mom, who worked for the Cohens, and he didn't want to separate us. But also partially because, even at that age, Mr. Cohen saw something in me that his own son lacked—and, even at that age, I was aware of what it was. Jack was smart, good-looking, athletic, outgoing and personable; he had everything in the world going for him except the ability to make an effort, to fix on something he wanted and go after it with single-minded determination. That was the quality I added to the equation—and, frankly, still did.

"*Focus*, Jack. We're talking about twenty million dollars and saving your family's bank, depending on how cooperative your dad and mom will be—" I'd tossed my duffle into the Porsche's trunk and held onto its door frame as I fell into the leather seat. "Shit, dude, I hate this car. I feel like I'm on the pavement."

He pushed the start button and the sound was like a jet readying for takeoff. "I love this car. I wouldn't drive anything else," he shouted back. I was jerked back into the seat as he pulled onto US 27 and pushed the engine to its limits. "I mean"—his forehead was furrowed as he rethought—"a Spyder, of course. That I'd drive. Now, a Spyder, that's the ultimate sexy ride! So, Clint buddy, did you have sex with this guy? Is that how you got his money?"

"Jesus, Jack. I don't do that anymore. I told you I gave up the escort business. Besides, I've been celibate for going on six months."

Jack turned his head to look at me—which was unnerving at the speed we were going—and put his right arm around the back of my neck to pull me over to him. "Come on, Clint, me, of all people. I'm the guy who knows you let the judge suck your cock and that's why you got a tiny little fine instead of ten years—"

"It wasn't a tiny little fine." Christ, how rich did you have to be to consider a hundred grand trivial? Seventy-five thousand of that had gone as directly into the pocket of the judge as my dick had in his mouth. I pushed Jack's hand off my neck. "You need to keep your fucking hands on the wheel and your eyes on the road if you're going to drive like Jeff Gordon."

Jack grinned. He was used to the rhythm of our friendship, even if it often irritated me. "Anyway, don't you think it's odd that a stranger would trust you with so much money?"

"It's not odd at all," I said, but I wanted to smack him. "I've run a very successful business *that I started all on my own,* unlike someone I know who had a family business handed to him—" I was about to explode. "Do you remember my years at Merril? My clients came in with a minimum of one million, and I made them even richer." Jack wasn't listening to me. He was racing with an older Cadillac, trying to catch the driver's eye to get him to take up Jack's offer of speed. "I have a knack for making people money, I set up limited partnerships for real estate and was able to retain ten percent of it for me, I've got a nice nest egg in those still!"

Jack turned and said, "Boring. You're always talking business."

"That's why your dad's always offering me a job at the bank. Both you and Abe want to sit back and enjoy the good life. I'm willing to bust ass."

Jack howled with laughter and placed his right hand on my thigh and squeezed it like it was a fresh orange. "And Alvaro knows you have friends in banking in the U.S."

"Yes," I admitted. "There is that."

"Then if your new fuck buddy can save the bank, I'm one hundred percent behind you. We all are."

"Go fuck yourself." I pushed his hand off my thigh and placed it back on the steering wheel.

Jack laughed again and faked holding the wheel tightly with both hands. "Is this OK for you, Grandpa?"

"If your family doesn't go along with this scheme you'll have to get used to driving a used truck."

The prospect of driving a used car got his attention. "Dad corralled Abe and me last night for a vigil at the Jewish Center, to ask for the right answer to the bank crisis. When we got home, you called. Mom has taken that as a sign you've got the answer we were looking for." He pushed the accelerator to the floor as we continued down Krome Avenue.

"What does Abe think?"

"Of you? Being involved with the family bank? He doesn't know. He thinks a few wealthy investors will do the trick. He's told Dad he's got some of our monied friends in Miami interested in it, but he's brought in nothing concrete so far."

I saw the speedometer hit a hundred as the stately palm trees whizzed by like cels in a cartoon. "He's going to be a problem."

Jack said, "I know." He reached over me to the glove compartment to fish out another cigarette. "Dad asked him to meet us at the bank, and he's going to be too curious not to come. Hell, he knows you're going to be there and he'll show up just for the opportunity to put you in your place one more time." I watched him light his Camel. "You're not going to tell him where your new business partner makes his money. Tell him he's an investor in some real estate deal you've got going in Mérida—that's where the money's coming from. But keep in mind"—he tossed the Dunhill lighter back in the glove compartment before slamming it shut again—"Mom and Dad are still the major shareholders in the bank, and by a long shot. Abe and I don't inherit a damned thing until one of them dies, God forbid, a hundred years from now." Jack took a long, slow drag and lowered his window before blowing the smoke out onto Krome Avenue. "Abe doesn't have the power to fuck this up. Do your best to keep him happy so he doesn't try and this doesn't get more complicated than it has to, but, at the end of the day, he doesn't have the power."

I smiled. Maybe Jack's powers of concentration were finally improving after all.

11

THE PORSCHE SQUEALED into the bank's parking lot. I knew that informing Abe of my coming involvement with his family's bank was necessary—as an officer of the bank he had access to its records and we couldn't simply allow twenty million to flow in unaccounted for—but meeting with him was going to be the most unproductive part of our day; it was, in fact, if you considered almost every other time Abe and I had met in our adult lives, going to be a brawl. Might as well get it over with sooner as later. I grabbed the door jamb to pull myself out of Jack's toy.

Jack's dad, David, had arrived, too, prompt as ever, directly from the tennis court from the look of him. He approached us from across the parking lot and, when he grabbed me for a solid hug, I could smell fresh-mowed grass on him.

"Good to see you, Clint, my boy!" He shook me a little during our embrace, and slapped my back before he released me. "After your nasty little legal issues here I worried I'd never see you again—and why would you come back to poor, old Homestead when you've got yourself all settled in a Mexican paradise!"

"To save your bank, David."

David was a good three decades older than me, forty pounds heavier, a full head shorter and with half my amount of hair on his pate, but I looked up to him as to no other man on earth. He was the only father-figure I could claim in my life. It felt very good to be able to say this to him.

David smiled at me and held open one of the bank's double front doors for Jack and me to pass through. The piped-in music in the bank's lobby was so somber it felt as if we were in a funeral home. And David spoke so softly we could, indeed, have been at a wake. "So, my boy, tell me how you plan on doing that?"

"In full detail, David. But let me tell you and Jack about it after we meet with Abe and he makes a run for it."

The board room at the main branch of Citizen's National Bank, where we were meeting, was done in the best of taste—polished chestnut wainscoting, original, brightly-colored modern art on the taupe grass-cloth wallpaper above, an oval conference table of solid mahogany, Italian leather chairs; I could see the hand of the elegant Candace in the details.

David stood at one end of the table, his hand in the pocket of his white tennis shorts, jiggling the car keys inside it. It was a nervous habit but one he'd had for so long that those of us who grew up around him weren't really bothered by it any longer. He started the meeting by providing a summary of where the bank stood, and how the purpose of our meeting could improve that standing, which boiled down to a few key concepts: This bank is in serious trouble; if we don't acquire more capital the Feds will take it over; my father started this bank in 1932 and I'll be damned if I'll let that happen.

Jack sat at the middle of the table, to his father's right. He kept his head down—the better to keep it out of Abe's line of fire—only nodding silently as his father made his points.

I sat on the other side of the table, opposite Jack, my Italian leather chair swiveled toward David, my face lifted as if I were enraptured by his words, my neck not turning no matter how many times Abe, who had taken a seat down at the other end of the table, opposite his father, declared his impatience by clearing his throat, or harrumphing, or slapping the table with his open palm. I didn't want to look at him because I was sure he would be wearing an idiot expression, breathing through his mouth, and such a show of stupid would piss me off. And because the flapping jowls he'd started to acquire in his late twenties, as he'd put on weight with alarming rapidity, were now so large they reminded me of an overfed hog and I didn't want to laugh in his face.

When David extended his hand to me, a gesture that he was turning over the floor, I nodded to him and addressed my comments to him, as if he were the only one in the room. "Thank you, David. It's good to be back home, and it's even better to be back with people I truly care about, my family in many ways, and to be able to offer you a proposition that could be so good for all of us. I've made a lot of money in the time I've been in Mexico—I've made some very good investments in real estate in Mérida and the surrounding areas which, as you all know, or should know, is a major tourist destination as well as one for well-to-do U.S. retirees. I need to get my money out of Mexico—I do a lot of charitable work there, but I have no interest in making its government one of my primary beneficiaries. You need to raise capital in order to keep the bank solvent and, as I understand it, you've already been looking for investors." I didn't turn to Abe even as I said this—even as I was fully aware that he was the one who'd come up with the plan to pursue investor capital in order to appease the Feds. I just kept talking. "I put myself forth as your investor—two million dollars"—and here I allowed myself a glance at my nemesis—"to start."

I saw Abe's jowls flap as he nodded, and a slight smile began to creep up his triple chin and into the only part of his face that wasn't fat, his nearly non-existent lips. I watched as it turned into a sneer. "I would rather see the bank get taken over by the Feds than sell any part of it to a cocksucker," he said.

The Cohen family was Jewish—not devout, by any means, but by heritage and tradition. I had been born of a Presbyterian mother, though I couldn't say I was "raised" in that tradition as, from an early age, I had spent much of my time with the Cohens and much of any religious learning I could claim had come over the Cohen dinner table, from David presenting us boys with ethical dilemmas and asking us to solve them. Abe was often frustrated by these conversations and asked to be excused from them; Jack most often took a backseat, keeping quiet while his father and I debated. When Abe was twenty-two he met a girl. She was from a Southern Baptist, Bible-thumping family and Abe was an enthusiastic convert to her faith. David told me, a few days after their wedding, that he felt as if he had lost a son. I often thought that Abe hadn't fallen in love with the girl so much as he'd fallen in love with the black-and-white answers of the easy, thoughtless theology she offered to him.

Now I swallowed hard as the word "cocksucker" seemed to reverberate crassly in the luxurious conference room. I saw Jack flinch, as if he wanted to react but was exerting control only in deference to his father's presence. David tugged on the keys in his pocket, so they jingled before he spoke. "Well, Abe, that's really my decision, isn't it? Who we sell the bank to. You're here as a courtesy. That's all."

Abe snorted. "Well, nice of you to invite me. But, Dad, you need to consider the ramifications of someone like Clint as an investor. It isn't going to sit well with our customers, letting some queer manage their money. It's a well-known fact that queers suck at money management and only a fool would—"

David took his hand out of his pocket and placed it on the top of the conference table. It was a gentle, graceful movement, but I could see the veins bulging on the top of it with the tension in David's body. "Abe," he said, "that's all. Meaning you can go. You now know my plan for the bank and there's no more reason for you to be here."

Abe snorted again, in disbelief, red rage rushing to fill out his flapping face. I wondered for a moment if he would do something truly Abe-like—bawl so loudly the nearby secretaries would come rushing into the room convinced of homicide, or pick up an edge of the table and flip it over. But Abe merely narrowed his eyes and spat at his father: "This is the most ungodly thing you have done in your whole godless life. If you go through with it, you will regret it."

David nodded. "There is always the possibility of regret, Abe, in almost everything one does in life," he said. And he kept a neutral expression on his face as Abe stormed from the room. When the sound of the door slamming behind Abe had evaporated, David at last took a seat and turned to me. "Now, Clint, tell me what the deal is. The real deal, not the bullshit you just fed my elder son."

12

I GRINNED; DAVID WAS still sharp as a fucking tack.

"I'll deposit twenty million dollars into your bank over the next several days. Sixteen of it, less bank fees, of course, will go into an account we'll open for my Mexican business partner, and four million of it will go into my existing account. I'll use two million of my cut to buy one half of the Cohen family's shares of the bank. And that really is just to start—money isn't an issue with my business partner..."

"Clint, my boy"—David laughed—"you're smart as they come, but no new business makes twenty million in just the few short months you've been in Mexico." He waved his fingers at me, an "out with it" gesture.

I looked toward Jack, but his head was still down. David waited patiently; I knew from long experience that if I tried to bullshit him he would know it. I swallowed, once but hard, before I spoke.

"My partner is a drug dealer. He makes his money in Mexico, and he needs to get it into the U.S. to protect it from being confiscated by his government. He deals mostly in cocaine, some weed. My guess is that meth is on the menu as well. As far as I understand it, he has little U.S. presence—he's not primarily a smuggler, I mean. He sells mostly to tourists in the Yucatan, and there's a steady local demand, too, of course. That's all I know."

David sighed, but he didn't flinch.

"Suppliers, like your friend," he said, "aren't the only ones who have to negotiate tricky federal rules and regulations in order to stay in business."

I nodded. "That was part of my thinking, too, when this deal was first presented to me."

The look in David's eyes was faraway. "How many millions, maybe billions, have I sent offshore to help my customers avoid the taxes?" It wasn't a question, so neither Jack nor I attempted to answer. "It'd be nice to bring some money *into* the country for a change."

Still, Jack and I waited.

Silence.

Watching David's mind work—the furrows of his brow deepened as he no doubt thought of the very real possibility he'd be the Cohen under whom a long-standing family business would have to close its doors, the son who couldn't sustain the father's legacy—I saw him wince. And my gut told me it was at that exact moment he was thinking about Abe, the utter arrogance of the root cause of their incredibly dire problems being the one to reject the solution I offered. We could hear, outside the door that Abe had so unceremoniously slammed, the muffled noises of a busy office in the middle of its morning—phones ringing, employees chatting as they walked down the hallway, the slow, steady hum of air conditioning, but around that table neither Jack nor I dared to make a sound while David thought through the option I had just offered up to him.

Suddenly, David rapped his knuckles on the top of the conference table and his eyes focused hard on mine. "How are we going to pull this off?" he asked.

Yes! This was a question I could answer. I spelled out my now well-considered theory. "Every bank has hundreds, possibly thousands, of dormant accounts—accounts that haven't been accessed in years because their owners are sick, or dead, or have simply forgotten about the account for one reason or another. I'll need a list of all the dormant accounts in the bank, ones with no activity for more than three years, but less than five. Five years and you're going to have to start contacting the accounts' owners and, if you can't find them, turn the funds over to the state. We need to hit that sweet spot: accounts that have been thoroughly abandoned but aren't old enough to be turned over."

"And we need these accounts... why?" David asked.

"Because no one ever pays attention to them—not the account owners; not the bank's accountants; not, for the most part, the Feds. We use them to receive wire transfers of funds from Mexico—odd amounts, not consistent, a few thousand or more per account. The money sits in the dormant account for a few hours, then it gets transferred out to my account and the new account we create for my partner."

David rapped the table again. "Transferred from where?"

"My bank in Mérida, where I will deposit it as cash into my personal account."

David's eyes went wide. "And this drug dealer trusts you to just take his cash from him and deposit it into your personal account? What stops you from just walking away with it? Twenty million, not peanuts!

How does he know you won't do that?" David shook his head. "How does he know some banker on this end won't do that?"

"He doesn't," I admitted. "But he knows that I'm aware he'll off me if he doesn't end up with access to his cash." I shrugged. "So, you see, I couldn't pull this off without you and Jack, without people I can trust entirely. I've got a lot of skin in the game."

David stood and paced the conference room. "And none of us—least of all Alvaro—could pull this off without you, Clint," he said at last. "Your scheme," he added, "is actually... genius."

13

DAVID AND I left Jack at the bank, bent over the tasks I'd asked of him: creating a list of accounts that had been dormant for over three years but shy of five, and then honing the list and dividing it into accounts of customers who were over eighty years old or dead, in nursing homes and/or suffering from dementia—those being the sort of customers who were not going to surprise us by looking for a strict accounting of their funds any time soon. Jack was to bring the lists to his parents' house when they were compiled—David and I were going there to have lunch with Candace—and I was looking forward to seeing them, not least because I was a Homestead native and I was curious to see if I recognized any of the names.

There was also the little matter of timing. The Feds, who'd been keeping tabs on the bank since Abe had brought the family business to their attention by making a bucketful of bad loans, would include the dormant accounts as part of their audits if there was suddenly a lot of activity on them. The good news was that the Feds were terribly predictable about when they would show up for the next round of audits. The bad news was that they were due back in four to six weeks, the last week of June at the latest. We either moved immediately or we waited another quarter for the federal auditors to clear out again—and a lot could happen in three months. Citizens National could collapse under the weight of its bad loans—bye-bye family business. I could be dead; I supposed making Alvaro wait for his money was likely not as lethal as stealing his money outright, but I didn't want to find out for sure—bye-bye me.

David slowed as we neared his house. He drove cautiously, like the banker he was. His BMW Seven Series smelled as if it had just arrived from Germany. "You know," he said, responding less to assuage his own raw nerves than to relieve mine and the tense silence between us, "I've had conversations before with two of the agents assigned to our bank. They've so much as said that if we can infuse more capital into the bank they really don't give a shit where it comes from." He cleared his throat—another nervous tick I was long familiar with; when we were kids, Jack and I laughed until *our* throats were raw that he wasn't going to be able to talk for a week, he'd cleared his throat so frequently the night we were twelve and he'd sat us down for the birds-and-bees talk. "Ours isn't the only banking institution that's in trouble with these loan issues. The political ramifications of bank failures would be unthinkable. If we can stabilize our situation, everyone will be happy."

"That's good to know, David."

"Just"—he cleared his throat again—"let's not be as forthcoming with Candy. She's an owner, of course, and I do want her to know we've found a way to get the bank back on solid footing—and she'll be thrilled that it's you who's going to be our partner... but I don't want her to know anything that's going to keep her up at night."

"Enough said, David," I told him as he turned into the driveway to his house, a curving fifty yards lined with tall palms and flanked by lush, manicured grass.

"Thanks, Clint."

"Don't mention it."

I saw him turn his head and grin at

me. "I won't mention it if you won't," he laughed.

14

"SON NUMBER THREE!" Candace greeted us by sailing down the ten front steps of the Cohens' Spanish-style spread, reminding me of that scene from *Funny Face* where Audrey Hepburn floats down two dozen steps, trailing red chiffon. Candace was trailing only green canvas gardening gloves and a pair of clippers—she'd been pruning the climbing pink roses that clung to the front archway when we drove up—and still she could have given Audrey a serious run for her money in the elegance department.

"Candy!" I called back, climbing out of the car and meeting her at the bottom step where she wrapped me in a hug and planted her lips all over my face.

"Well, hello, honey,"—she held me at arm's length now to get a good look at me—"what a pleasure to see you!" I loved the soft,

Carolina accent that added so much to the woman's charm. "Clearly something important going on for you and David to show up together!" She raised her eyebrows at her husband and they pecked each other on the cheek as he moved past us, up the stairs and into the house. She turned back to me, eyebrows still anxious. "Is everything all right in Mexico?"

"Better than I ever expected it could be," I assured her.

"As I've been led to believe," she said, threading her arm through mine as we followed behind her husband. "I hear you've made yourself a real estate mogul, south of the border." She led me in through the house's large double doors, down a hallway and past a winding, wrought-iron staircase flanked by two huge living rooms, one on either side, both equally beautiful in their Spanish-elegance-meets-Florida bright charm, and both invitingly comfortable, continuing on through a formal dining room and directly into the kitchen, where David was pouring Scotch into Waterford tumblers.

"I've managed to do well for myself," I conceded, swelling with pride at the accolades but not wanting to go into too much detail about so much non-existent real estate. I was willing to hedge with Candace but I didn't want to put myself into the position where I'd be offering her an outright lie. And the best way to keep her from asking too many questions was to change the subject. "I've done so well, as a matter of fact, that I've told David I'd like to put some of my money into the bank…"

I looked quickly at David to make sure that he was comfortable with the direction I was going. He nodded and grinned without parting his lips. Then he tossed a few ice cubes into one of the glasses before he poured the Scotch, making Candace wince. "I know, dear," David smiled fully now, "just spring water for you." He waggled the bottle of Scotch at me and said, "Eighteen-year-old single malt. Candace thinks I'm a criminal for drinking it on the rocks," by way of explanation.

"I want to issue an indictment every time he does it," Candace confirmed.

"Ice for you?" David asked me.

"I wouldn't dare," I said, and Candace patted my cheek in approval.

David handed out the libations, raising his as if in a toast, and we all clinked before we sipped.

Candace lowered her glass and set it on the granite kitchen counter, pursing her lips slightly to repair any smudge of her bright red lipstick the sip might have caused, and looked at me. "David doesn't sleep at night, worried about that damned bank. Your offer is a godsend," she said simply.

I grinned, and I think I blushed a little. There was so much pleasure in Candace's approval—as there always had been for me, and Jack, and David.

David took another sip of his Scotch. "Abe's not completely on board."

"Well, then..."—Candace smiled sweetly, letting the Carolina in her voice thicken into syrup—"screw him. I think it's a little more than ironic that the person who caused all this trouble for the bank with his poor choices thinks he can stand in the way of solving the problem." She took her glass with her and moved to the small, floral-covered loveseat tucked in the breakfast nook, where she took a regal seat and crossed her legs. "Just, you know... *fuck him.*"

Candace whipped up a shrimp salad for our lunch after Jack arrived with the lists I'd asked him for—lists he'd carefully winnowed, names and account numbers he'd uploaded to a memory stick and slipped to me out of his mother's line of vision. I tucked the little gadget discreetly into the back pocket of my shorts. He and I loaded our plates first with the salad, crusty rolls, and sliced mangoes Candace was serving to us. I took the opportunity, while we waited on the small patio outside the breakfast nook for his parents to join us, to quiz him on Candace's uncharacteristic outburst—I mean, I'd heard Candace curse before; she was a woman with strong opinions, after all—but her flat and furious dismissal of her first born... that was new. "Really, Jack. What's up with that?"

Jack shrugged. "She feels as if she lost him when he married that girl and took up with the fundamentalists. She can't understand that way of thinking, that way of life, at all. And she truly, truly dislikes the wife who is, in all fairness to my mom, absolutely clueless."

We both took a bite of the open-faced sandwiches we'd made—which were awesome—and Jack thought as he chewed. When he'd swallowed he continued: "As an example, the wife—"

"'The wife'?" I laughed. "What's her name?"

"Ahhhh," Jack stalled, thinking, "Sharon! But we don't use it. The wife cornered Mom at a cocktail party about a year ago and admired the diamond necklace she was wearing. Mom thanked her for the compliment, but the wife went on, something on the order of she was looking forward to inheriting all Mom's beautiful jewelry someday because, God knew, Abe's queer little brother wasn't ever going to get married so there wasn't going to be another girl in the family to give them to..."

"You're kidding!"

"Not kidding. Just so wrong on so many levels..."

"So very, very many levels..."

"Needless to say the jewels are all being left to me—Mom put it in her will the next day, so be nice to me..."

"In case I'm in want of a diamond necklace someday?"

"You never know." We laughed and he took another bite of his sandwich. "Anyway," he said, speaking through his shrimp, "I've already had a call from Abe about our deal, trying to shut it down."

"To be expected, correct?"

"Of course. The asshole."

"And here I thought Southern Baptists were all about honoring thy father and thy mother."

Jack snorted. "He could cause a lot of trouble if he wanted to, but I'm actually not that worried about Abe." He glanced up to make sure his parents weren't about to make their entrance onto the patio. "There are some fairly substantial rumors circulating that Abe has a girlfriend—"

I almost choked. "Your holier-than-thou brother is screwing around on his legally Christian wife?"

"That's the scuttlebutt. And, believe me, if the wife gets wind of it she will cut him out of her life so fast his head will fly off his shoulders—and she will clean him out in the process." He nodded. "No pre-nup. If I hint to Abe that the wife might somehow get wind of the girlfriend, that'll do for damage control."

"I thought her religion didn't allow for divorce?"

"Her religion is money, my friend. Her own, private religion is all about the big bucks."

I smiled at my lifelong friend. "You are ruthless."

He smiled back. "A ruthless *genius*, please."

"An *evil genius*," I countered and Jack let out a villainous "Bwah-ha-ha!"

David and Candace finally joined us on the patio, David carrying a chilled and already-opened bottle of Napa Valley sauvignon blanc and four stemmed glasses. "Candace liked this wine so much when we were in Yountville last year she bought six cases," he told us as he poured. Then, considering, he added, "In fact, Candace found so many wines she liked on that trip I damned near had to expand the wine closet to hold everything she had shipped home."

Candace smiled sweetly and said, "Don't exaggerate, darling." Turning to me she asked, "Now, Clint, tell me, is there anything we can do to expedite our partnership? I'm looking forward to having you in the fold, so what do we need to do at our end?"

I smiled, the stick of lists secure in my back pocket, and told Candace, "Nothing more that I can think of. When I get back to Mexico I'll tell my banker, a fellow named Juan Carlos, to make the transfer of money—and considering that I'll be paying his bank a hefty fee for the work I'm sure he'll make it happen quickly. I'll be in touch with Jack to make him aware the money is on its way and to keep an eye out..." I shrugged, to convey to Candace that my ownership in the bank was a *fait accompli* as far as I was concerned. "I'm flying back this evening, and it's all up to me at this point—"

David interrupted. "For my part, because I'm sure there's going to be no issue with the transfer, I'll call our attorneys this afternoon and have the necessary paperwork drawn up so it'll be ready for our signatures when you return to Miami."

Candace clapped her hands just once with delight. "Perfection. I love all my men working together like this! But tell me when that will be, Clint—when will you be returning to Miami? We must have a party to celebrate, and you've got to give me a bit of time to plan."

"I'm not exactly sure, Candace," I told her, and grinned because I knew she was going to eat this next part up: "The partner I told you about? My partner in Mexico?"

"Yes?" She stretched the word into four expectant syllables, onto an upcoming surprise.

"He's a businessman by day, and a bullfighter by night—or, I should say, on the weekends during the off season—"

Candace drew in her breath audibly. "Are you kidding me?"

"I am not."

"That's simply too wonderful!"

"I've been invited to his next fight, which is taking place in just a little under two weeks, and of course I can't miss it, and I need to coordinate my schedule—"

"David?" Candace cut me off, turning to her husband.

"Yes, my dear?"

"I've never seen a bullfight."

David nodded with the resolve common to men who've lived their lives with strong-willed women. "Are we going to Mexico, my dear?"

"Of course we are. Clint, you let us know when that fight is to take place and David will book our tickets, and—"

It was my turn to jump in: "You're business partners now with a young man who has access to his associate's private jet. You cannot possibly fly commercial."

Candace laughed. "I wouldn't think of it. But"—she held up one, long manicured finger—"I can think of something that David and I can do to return the favor. How would you like to give your business partner a gift that will be the highlight of his year?" I started to respond, but she waggled the elegant finger. "Let me make a phone call..."

Half an hour later, as we were finishing a second bottle of Candace's favorite sauvignon blanc, I heard a car pull into the Cohens' driveway, coughing and knocking as it chugged up the long path to the house. "What in heaven's name—" I blurted, but I saw David and Candace exchange a look, and David rose to make his way to the kitchen door.

"Out on the patio, Chester," he called.

Chester appeared at the door that David held open for him so he could join us outdoors. He had a round face, deeply tanned like the rest of his body and deeply grooved. He looked older than he seemed from the spring in his step, probably from working outside most of his life. At least I assumed so from the thin blue workpants and shirt

84

and the scuffed and muddied boots he wore, but, clearly, from the way that he and David were embracing, and that Candace rose to allow him to kiss her on the cheek, he was far more than the family's gardener or handyman.

Chester was followed in the door by the loveliest creature I had ever seen—abundant dark, shiny hair with black eyes framed by lashes so thick they could have caused a Nor'easter when she batted her eyes, and a wiry, girlish body. She looked eighteen but, from the way she carried herself, I thought she must be older than that, if not by much.

Chester carried a box in his arms, the sort a department store might have used to deliver a dress to the home of a wealthy patron in a more gracious decade, and just as gray with the stain of dust. When David and Candace had thoroughly greeted him—and Jack, too, had risen to give him a hug—David winked at me and said, "Clint, you remember our dear friend, Chester Cruet. Chester, you remember Clint Kennedy. And this is Charlotte, Chester's daughter."

Charlotte laughed, to my ears the sound of an angel who'd been ever so slightly amused. "Daddy's chauffer today, I think."

"A loyal employee of the bank," David clarified, putting an arm around her thin, bronzed shoulders, "though she's attending college—doesn't want to be a banker, don't ask me why when she's already got a job for life, if only she wants it."

Charlotte smiled at her employer, vaguely irritated by his introduction but graciously allowing his arm to continue to rest across her shoulders.

"Mr. Kennedy," Chester said and approached me, holding the box toward me. "I have brought you a gift."

I looked at each of the Cruets, hoping for a clue, reluctant to remove my eyes from the redoubtable Charlotte, but I took the box and carefully lifted the lid. "Oh! Oh, Chester!"

Inside the box was a red satin cape, slightly discolored and more than a little wrinkled from its years in the old box, its shoulders thickly embroidered in gold thread, its collar dense with golden studs and seed pearls.

"It belonged once to Ernesto Pastor," Chester told me, "the greatest Puerto Rican *torero* of all time—a friend of my grandfather's—"

I gasped again. "Chester, how... how can I ever repay you for this?"

Chester put his hands up to stop me. "It is my pleasure. Candace told me that you are helping David out with the bank situation. It gives me great happiness, then, to help you."

I'm the sort of person who is rarely speechless, but I wasn't sure what was choking me up more at the moment—Chester's generosity, Charlotte's beauty, or that Candace was able to make one phone call and within half an hour put a cape into my hands that had once belonged to Ernesto Pastor.

15

Jack drove me back to the airport. He lit up a cigarette as soon as he put the car in gear, lowered the driver's window with his left hand, enough to suck out the smoke, and tapped the console with his right. "In there," he said, exhaling.

In the console was a stack of signature cards. "Sign two of them. To open Alvaro's new account—I'm guessing you won't mind a little forgery in the midst of all of this?"

If Alvaro had thought through this detail of the plan my guess is it would make him batshit crazy—I, myself, wouldn't sleep well knowing that twenty million dollars of my money was in the bank based on someone else's imitation of my John Hancock. On the other hand, I didn't have a couple dozen armed thugs ready to take out any pest who fucked me over. "Don't mind if I do," I told Jack.

I signed the cards with Jack's Montblanc. Outside the Porsche's window the old homes of the first homesteaders receded to a blur as we sped by. My grandparents' home was one of those, built in 1902. Cubans lived in the house now, chain link surrounding the front ten acres. Pigs, horses, and chickens ran freely inside the fence. None of the old orange or grapefruit groves remained. A few days ago I would have thought I'd gone about as far from that old bungalow as it was possible to get; now, the possibilities that had opened up to me since my meeting with Alvaro would stagger the current inhabitants. A few days ago I would have thought I'd done well enough for myself to make David Cohen as proud a father as a man could be; now, the reality that I was about to save David's bank staggered *me*.

Jack interrupted my reverie. "If your banker—Juan Carlos, you called him? If he isn't cooperative, I'm thinking, I mean, since Alvaro's jet already has clearance for customs, you could bring the cash in by air. We could send the armored car out to the airport to pick it up, divide it up among our eight branches just in case anyone takes a close look..." He drove with one hand on the wheel and flicked the spent cigarette out the window.

I nodded. "Always good to have options, Jackie. Let's stick with wiring it into the inactive accounts, for the time being." I stuffed the signed cards back into the console. "I'm thinking, given the number of accounts we can use, our capacity's going to be about a million a day, max, but maybe if you could divide up the accounts among the branches, I mean eight different accounts for each inactive customer, we could step up the amount we're transferring, get the whole amount into the bank faster?"

Jack frowned—"Could be tricky..."—but he didn't dismiss the idea out-of-hand.

We drove for a few miles in silence, as Jack thought through my latest suggestion.

"Hey, Jack?"

"Yeah?"

"What's the low-down on Chester's daughter?"

"Charlotte?"

I nodded.

He thought for a moment. "Smart. The hardest working person at the bank, *and* she goes to night school. Dad had her following Abe around for a while, you know, to keep him in line, and she did such a good job of it he made her his secretary. And"—he grinned at me—"way above your pay grade, pal."

Workers on the ground pulled the stairs away, the jet's door swung shut automatically and sealed, and Tim locked it manually. "Alvaro's been calling all afternoon," he told me, "wanting to know if you were back yet, so I called him when I saw you drive up and told him we were on our way." I nodded to acknowledge him, scrolling through my phone to find Juan Carlos's number.

"Anything I can get you, before we start to taxi?" he asked. I frowned, thinking how sated I felt from Candace's splendid shrimp salad and good wine and the magnitude of the deal I had just negotiated with such breathtaking ease. I waved Tim away and he gave me a look of grave disappointment.

"Maybe a glass of water," I relented. "Once we're in the air." I'd had a lot to drink, a busy day behind me and it wasn't over yet, and who knew what awaited me tomorrow; I truly didn't want to deal with the effects of dehydration. "Juan Carlos? Are you able to meet me at my house tonight? Two hours, I think—make it three to be safe. I'm leaving Miami now."

Tim shrugged as the engines hummed and quickly revved up. Within thirty seconds we'd lifted off the pavement and I heard the bump of the wheels being stowed, some of the wine glasses in the galley tinkling as we angled up for altitude. When we banked left as we passed over the town, I could see a branch of the bank below. *My* bank.

Tim served me sparkling water with a slice of lime in a heavy-bottomed tumbler as we flew over Key West. I saw a little bit of Cuba in the distance and I looked down at the ocean as we headed to the Yucatan— beautiful, wide-open blue waters, dotted with just a few scattered sailboats on unknown journeys. I would be a multi-millionaire within the month.

16

W E TOUCHED DOWN and the reverse thrust-ers kicked in, the taxi lights shimmer-ing across the broken concrete runway as the plane taxied toward Alvaro's hanger. We sluggishly pulled inside the hanger and I heard the tires squeal on the pristine Italian tile floors. When the engines shut down, the only sound was Alvaro's angry voice echoing in the open space, sputtering loudly into his cell phone: "I don't give a fuck... A *fuck*! You tell him he takes ten from me, I will have twenty back! Fuck! Forty back, you tell the ungrateful little motherfuck from me—"

I sighed. I had no idea who Alvaro was talking to but he was very clearly on the oth-er side of cocktail hour. I clutched my duf-fle and held the department store box under one arm, while Tim stood next to me at the galley, waiting for the airport attendant to signal to the pilot to open the door and drop the stairs. I wanted to ask him, "Does he do this often? Just how much does Alvaro drink and how often does he go off the rails like that?" but thought better of it. For one thing, I really didn't want to know the specifics; I already understood it was going to be hard to handle him. Instead, I offered, "Thanks for taking such good care of me, Tim. I think I'm going to be a regular passenger over the next few weeks and I really appreciate it."

Tim took the hand I'd extended to him and leaned forward, too close to my face for my comfort. "I'll look forward to that." Thankfully, the airport attendant signaled and the pilot opened the cockpit door to tell Tim to open the door.

Alvaro was up the stairs and inside the plane before Tim had finished the job, brushing past him to grab me and hug me like I was a POW coming home. "A drink to celebrate!" he ordered Tim, who rushed to obey, not breaking his stride even when Alvaro slapped him on his ass.

"Yes, sir," Tim replied.

I checked the time on my phone and sighed again as I set my duffle and my dusty box on one of the long white leather sofas and took a seat. I didn't know if Tim was one of Alvaro's toys—although that was certainly looking more true than not—but I had no intention of confirming my suspicions this evening in some three-way fantasy Alvaro had dreamed up; I was due to meet Juan Carlos within the half hour. Tim materialized again with a silver ice bucket, a bottle of vodka, and two crystal tumblers on a silver tray. "Anything else I can get you gentlemen?" he asked, and winked. I was suddenly overcome with my own fantasies: slipping a mickey into Alvaro's vodka, if only I had a mickey handy. How did a man get to be a dangerous drug kingpin with twenty million dollars floating around in small bills when he was so unfocused on taking care of business?

"Yes," Alvaro said and my heart sank at the thought of what he might have on his vodka-addled mind. "Some cheese and crackers, and some green olives on the side." Alvaro turned to me. "So, Clint, your trip went well?"

"It went better than I could have hoped," I told him, sighing again with what a more astute or less drunk person would have realized was relief.

He'd taken a seat on the opposite sofa, directly across from me, his legs spread wide, his elbows resting on his knees so he could lean close to me, his glass of vodka in one hand, dangling between his thighs. "Clint, my partner, give me details!" he demanded and laughed.

Which was exactly what I didn't want to do. I didn't want him to know how easy it had been for me to have Jack transfer all the information we needed onto a little stick smaller than a box of matches and resting now in my back pocket. And I surely didn't want to tell him about the drama Abe had created, which would worry him. My idea to use the dormant accounts had been, indeed, as David had pointed out, a stroke of genius, but there was no need for Alvaro to know how impressively brilliant I was.

"Can we meet with your banker tonight?" he asked. "I have never made the acquaintance of Juan Carlos..."

It took all my self-control not to flinch. How did he know my banker's name? What did he know of the arrangements I'd made with him? Had he tapped my phone? Did he have an inkling that he would double-cross me—that if he possessed the little stick in my back pocket he could conceivably take it to Juan Carlos himself and cut me out of the deal? Not bloody likely to happen. David was loyal and would never allow it, and Alvaro wasn't smart enough to figure out such a scheme on his own and find another U.S. partner.

"I'm not meeting with anyone tonight, Alvaro. I've had a hellishly long day and I've got to get an early start tomorrow to take care of your business, so tonight I'm going home and taking a shower and going to bed."

I watched his black eyes as he looked out the window. He wiped the sweat from his tumbler of ice and vodka on his black jeans. I waited for him to look at me and, when several minutes passed with no indication that this was going to happen, I decided my phone was secure after all and tapped the dusty box. "The only other thing I'm going to do tonight is give you a present."

This captured his interest.

I had planned to present the cape to Alvaro with more ceremony, at some more celebratory juncture, but a diversionary tactic in hand is worth two in the bush and so I picked up the box and placed it on the coffee table between us—just as Tim returned with the tray of snacks Alvaro had ordered, flummoxed about where to put it down as the box took up every inch of the table save for what was in use by the silver drink tray.

Alvaro, his black eyes shining now with anticipation, waved the steward away. "For me?"

"For you."

Alvaro reached out with both hands to lift the lid.

"It once belonged to Ernesto Pastor."

"No," Alvaro breathed. He floated one hand on top of the red satin, as if it was too precious a relic to handle. His hand hovered for several seconds, as his black eyes brimmed, and then he very slowly lifted the cape from its resting place. The satin crinkled as it unfolded, and Alvaro rose as he pulled it from its box and extended it to its full length. Dust motes swirled around its gilded shoulders, tickling my nose, but Alvaro was oblivious to anything but the cloth's beauty, and its history. He stood, mouth agape, in awe at what he held in his two hands, for at least a full minute. I was afraid he was going to whip the cape around him in one of his signature flourishes, treatment I wasn't sure the fragile fabric could withstand, but all he did was lovingly lower the cape back into the box, careful to replicate its original folds, and then he reached for his glass. "I trust you, Clint," he said, holding the glass up to me. "I am beginning to see you wouldn't do anything that would require me to harm you."

I held my glass up and clinked it with his. "Here's to a long and profitable partnership," I said, and we both drank.

"Now, Alvaro, do you want to give me a ride home or should I call my houseboy?"

17

MY HOUSEBOY, PEDRO, opened the iron entrance gate with one hand, the other reaching for my duffle, both eyes on the Hummer that was dropping me off and the gorgeous man I'd been sitting next to in the back seat. "Very nice, Mister Clint. Is he your new friend?"

Thankfully, I'd been facing Pedro as he spoke and no one in the Hummer saw my eyes rolling around in their sockets in a silent but explicit answer to him of "No, absolutely the fuck not." I got control of my ocular muscles again before I turned around, briefly, to wave at Alvaro as the Hummer pulled away from the curb. The only one who could really fuck up this deal was the one who stood to benefit most, and I watched him drive away with a smile slapped on my face.

Angry and shaken, I went directly to my bedroom and jumped into the shower. Pedro furnished me with a warm towel and clean clothes—a fresh pair of jeans and a Hard Rock Café pullover—and I was ready when Juan Carlos showed up at my front door, exactly on time.

"Hello, Juan Carlos!" I met him in the foyer with a hug—not your common business greeting, except among those of us who have the need to check for wires before we can talk freely. Juan Carlos, after a slight and natural hesitation, hugged me in return, his nonchalance almost as much assurance as the sweep my hands managed of his body that he was clean.

"Your home is beautiful," Juan Carlos told me as we walked through the foyer, his head swiveling back on his neck to take in the eighteen-foot plaster ceilings and crown moldings. "We Mexicans are happy to see the Americans come in and restore these old colonial houses. Most of my people want to be out in the new suburbs, away from the old city."

"I can't imagine why." I offered him a seat on a sofa in my living room. "I bought this place three years ago, when I realized I wanted to live in the Yucatan permanently, at some point. Started restoration as soon as escrow closed. Took me almost two years to finish—I hired a local architect and local workers, very talented but with an exasperating sense of what a full work day entails. Anyway"—I took a seat on the sofa opposite Juan Carlos—"I love it and I can't imagine living in the suburbs. Give up all of this artisan beauty"—I indicated the plaster finish on the walls, the colorful tile floors, the polished mahogany doors—"for what? Shoddy new construction, not to mention tiny rooms and claustrophobically low ceilings—"

"I live in the suburbs, Señor Kennedy."

I nodded; of course he did. I took in his rumpled, inexpensive suit, his Casio watch, his loafers, highly polished but in need of new heels. All of it screamed mid-level banker; where else would he live but in a three-bedroom, two-and-a-half bath split-level, probably in want of an owner who had a better understanding of deferred maintenance? It wasn't that I minded the cheapness, but the lack of care and the absolute void of originality made me weary. "I didn't mean *you*, of course," I said, and smiled—genuinely smiled; I did not want to piss him off, he was a vital link in my chain. I sat back on my sofa, still smiling, awkwardly aware that I had probably offended him, and waited for his return fire. He'd been so accommodating yesterday when I'd phoned from the Cohens' to first bring this deal to his attention, and now I waited for him to find fault with it. To ask uncomfortable questions of his own about the origins of the money slated for transfer. He had to know we were dealing with drug money; millions in cash weren't going to be sitting around from saved up paychecks. Had I just handed him an excuse to wash his hands of it, and me? To keep his hands clean?

Instead, Juan Carlos reached into his breast pocket and drew out a spiral notebook and a short pencil that looked as if he'd appropriated it the last time he'd played a round of golf, and sat back on the sofa scratching some figures on one of the sheets. "How much money are we talking about—to help me to calculate my percentage."

It was unlike me to have underestimated the allure of profit.

"Twenty million, to start. One million on Day One. There'll be more if all the details of this first transfer fall into place."

"Very good, Señor Kennedy. And the details? What are they?"

I sat up and leaned forward. "I want to get started on the transfers as quickly as we can—tomorrow, if possible. I have over two hundred accounts in the U.S. that can each receive a wire, in increments of no more than $9,900." I reached into the back pocket of my jeans, where I'd transferred the memory stick after stepping into my fresh clothes, and handed it to him. "I want to use the first one hundred and two on the spreadsheet first—names, account numbers, bank routing number, it's all on there." Juan Carlos reached out for the stick, but I gripped it tighter. "All one hundred and two tomorrow." At that rate, it would take twenty business days to transfer the twenty million into the states; in less than a month I would be the owner of four million dollars.

I released my hold and Juan Carlos accepted the gadget, frowning. "It's a lot of work for that many accounts"—I could see the calculations going on behind his pale, hazel eyes: what two percent added up to in terms of bank fees that could translate into a promotion at the bank for bringing in new business of such magnitude, a happy wife ordering a new tile floor for their half bath, his aching feet in a new pair of loafers—"but I can do a lot of it tonight from home. In the morning I will send our armored car to you to collect the money and begin the transfers. Since this will be the first time we're doing it, I suggest we transfer into only three or four accounts and then verify the U.S. account received it."

I put out my hand. "Agreed. I'll be ready at nine AM."

Juan Carlos offered me his damp hand

in return, then I escorted him to my front door and watched him walk down the street to his twenty-year-old Chevy. The car door creaked as he opened it. This was not the very picture of a man who was going to have millions of dollars running through his short, damp, little fingers in the morning—short, damp, little *suburban* fingers caressing all those fives, tens and twenties, fifties and hundred-dollar bills that had been scrunched in the paws of drug users eager for their next high, their next fix. The smelly, damp drug cash stored at Alvaro's house. The Chevy started and it sounded as if two cylinders were retired. When he drove past me a trail of smoke floated gently down to the asphalt road.

There were two messages on my phone, one from Alvaro and one from Jack. I called to Pedro to bring me a Sol, walked out to my pool and slumped down on a lounge chair while I dialed Jack back.

"When can we start?" Jack asked.

"Hello to you, too."

"Hello. When can we start?"

"My guy's doing the computer work tonight, and the car will be here to transport the money at nine." I took a swig of my beer. "They'll have to count it, of course, but I think you should start checking the accounts by noon, at least, and call me as soon as it starts to flow. My guy will take his cut right off the top so just dump a straight twenty percent into my account and the rest into Alvaro's."

Jack let out a whoop, and I could envision him pumping the air with his fist. "Smooth, Clint," he laughed.

"How's Abe? Heard from him?"

"Dad did. But he handled him, asked him if he was dating anyone we knew and that shut dear big brother right up—and he didn't tell him anything about the transfers. By the time Abe finds out it'll be a done deal. If Abe's our biggest problem, we're home free."

"Easy for you to say, Jackie. You're not the one who has to drive a million bucks in small bills to the bank tomorrow."

"The greater the risk, the greater the reward."

I took another swig of my beer. "Preaching to the choir, brother."

Pedro had turned on the pool and garden lights and my terrace looked like a resort, palms gently swaying and the tiniest of movement on the surface of the water. I heard the mariachi players from the park just six blocks away, filled with the local people out for the evening. I dialed Alvaro.

"Hello, Clint, my partner!" He laughed—clearly he'd had a few more drinks since I'd left him, but he was in a good mood and I figured that was a plus.

"I've been thinking about logistics—"

"Yes, partner, I have, too. The money is all counted and packed in suitcases—"

"Good, good. Drive one million to my house in the morning—have it here by nine."

The silence on the other end of the line was suddenly very sober. "Why your house? Why don't we go directly to the bank?"

"Because it's more discreet my way. If I arrange for the bank's armored car to pick it up I'll be able to give you a receipt for it—I mean, do you want to walk in the bank with all those suitcases of cash and ask for a voucher? Or have a bunch of uniformed guards who don't answer to you in your house, counting the money and hauling out the suitcases in front of your kids? If you do, I'm happy to change the plan..."

"No, no, no. Your way is good. But what do I do about your receipt, Clint?"

"My receipt?"

"I give you my money and you give it to the bank... where is my receipt from you?"

"We've already talked about this, Alvaro. My life is my receipt, because if I don't do right by you, you will have my life."

The drunken laugh Alvaro let out in response was, actually, terrifying.

"Also, Alvaro? I want two of your guards to stay at my house while the money's counted, until the bank takes it away. This is additional insurance for you of my honesty—"

"You are not a stupid man, Clint. I wanted you because you are a person to get things done. From everything I know, you honor your word, no matter what." I heard the ice clink as he took another sip of his vodka, and then he repeated, "You are not a stupid man."

Of course not, I thought; this way, if it turned out Juan Carlos had set me up and things went south, Alvaro's men—and Alvaro—would bear the brunt of scrutiny for the crime. I wouldn't be off the hook completely in that case, but in terms of the usual suspects, I was going to be able to wiggle out of legal trouble a whole lot more easily if I had Alvaro's men—and their kingpin—to link to the money. "Thank you," I said.

I finished my drink and rolled up the legs of my jeans and put my feet in the cool water of the pool. The breeze made slight waves skitter across the surface, to the tile borders, light flickering off the wavelets like a bed of sparkling diamonds.

18

COFFEE. EVERYONE OF them wanted a cup: Alvaro's four men, the two bank guards, the accountant who came to count the money, the driver of the armored car; milk, cream, sugar, Stevia, *honey*, for Christ's sake—they kept Pedro hopping, whistling as he worked, possibly a Mayan morning prayer, a soothing sound almost like a meditation. I detected the faint aroma of pot, a drug I no longer indulged in, permeating the money and seeping from it into the living room until I felt the vague, slothful presence of a contact high. Even so, Alvaro and his men had done an admirable job on their count and by 9:40 I was handing his thugs a receipt for an even one million big ones and settled in my car, following an armored car to the offices of Banco de Mexico.

I took the ten-minute drive to Juan Carlos's office in silence—no radio, no phone, the only sound the smooth hum of my Land Rover's engine. I watched as an old man moved in slow steps lugging a five-gallon bucket of water that he would use to clean the sidewalks. A boy of six or seven, likely the grandson of the sidewalk cleaner, walked beside him, keeping pace and carrying a broom with thick yellow bristles. Shop owners were on the sidewalks hosing down awnings or washing display windows with squeegies or shoveling debris from the night before out of their gutters. The godly people of Mérida, a city noted for its cleanliness, looked up when the armored car ahead of me passed by, as if it might contain the Pope come to bestow a blessing.

Juan Carlos occupied a windowless office on the third floor of the bright white bank building on Reforma Street. He was even more rumpled than he'd been at my house the night before, showing the effects of no sleep and a long night of tedious work. His office was painted plain white, furnished with an old-fashioned metal desk and devoid of personal effects, but I was mightily impressed when he told me he was prepared, at that very moment, to begin to wire Alvaro's money—and that he believed the whole of the first million could be transferred within two short hours.

I grinned. "Let's go."

At my direction, Juan Carlos tapped a single key on his computer keyboard, then sat back in his armless swivel chair and crossed his arms.

I looked at him. "Have you done it?"

"Yes," he said, and nodded.

"That's it?"

"You might want to call your friend in Miami and see if the money has yet made it into his bank. Tell him to look at the account of a gentleman named Elmer Collier."

I pulled my cell from my shirt pocket. No beeps or blips, no flashing lights, not even a flicker? Worse, I knew Elmer Collier. His youngest grandson had been one of my boys back in my escort days, and I'd actually given the kid a ride to the nursing home to visit Elmer a few times. Elmer was then ninety-three years old, lying on a bed covered with plastic sheets so he wouldn't piss all over the nursing home's mattress and ruin it. He'd been a janitor at the prep school Jack and I had attended, always walking with his head down, broom or mop in hand and trailing a big orange bucket on wheels, slopping water in his wake.

It all seemed terribly anticlimactic. "Jack?"

"Hey! Clint! Where are you? Dad and I are at the bank—he's in his office pacing

and jangling his keys, and I'm in the kitch-
en, making us coffees. We're ready when you
are—"

"Jack, go into your office and check Elmer Collier's account."

"Fuck— You started—"

"Yeah. Call me back when you get to
your office."

"Fuck, no, hold on, hold on..."

I held on, listening to Jack's footfalls on
the deep carpeting in the bank's hallway, the
door to his private office closing behind him,
his fingers tapping on a distant computer
keyboard.

"Fuck, Clint..."

"What?" I asked, clutching my phone,
waiting to hear the worst, bracing myself to
be told it couldn't be this easy to undermine
the tax entities, drug enforcement agencies,
and financial regulations of two countries.

"It's here. Nine thousand and nine hundred brand new dollars in Elmer Collier's account. Hey... wait a minute. Elmer Collier?
Don't we know him?"

19

'M NOT A student of human nature; I'm a natural. I've spent so much time in my life sizing people up to find out which ones were best suited—and most ably disposed—to helping me meet my goals that I can spot a mark, a dick, a pussy, or a sociopath before I can see the whites of their eyes. But Alvaro? I grew increasingly uncomfortable with each phone call, each time I called him or he called me—which he must have done twenty times during the course of the day, while the transfers were happening—with each escalating display of glee I heard on the phone when another, and then another, and then another of the wires had made it into their targeted dormant account. I didn't begrudge him the calls, on the face of it, of course; it was his million dollars—the two hundred thousand of it that wasn't mine, that is—

and he had a right to be concerned about its disposition. What was throwing me were the squeals, the way he grew to sound more and more like an excited piglet through the course of the day. The ruthless, intimidating drug kingpin I could deal with; the five-year-old on too much sugar was not in my wheelhouse.

I left the bank at 2:30 that afternoon, after all the day's transfers were complete, one cool million stashed neatly in two brand new Miami accounts, and headed straight to Alvaro's hacienda. I'd hoped that seeing him in the flesh would allay some of the fears that had been building during the course of the day—voices on the telephone can be as deceiving and as easily misinterpreted as e-mails or text messages, or at least that was how I consoled myself. My hopes were high as the guards waved me through the electronic gates at Alvaro's estate, but after I parked my car and sprinted into the central courtyard and saw Alvaro standing by the pool, flipping steaks at a flaming grill with one hand and waving a tumbler of tequila in the other, wearing nothing but a pair of tight, white underwear—my heart sank. Don't get me wrong, Alvaro looked mighty fine in his underwear—slim waist, firm shoulders, a fair amount of hair on his thick legs and more than his fair share of bulge in the crotch. I fully understood why my boys used to compete with each other when he phoned in for a date. While it may at first glance seem counterintuitive, however, people who run escort services are the ones who most fully and sincerely understand the concept of not shitting where one eats. That is, we know that if your business is fucking, then you don't fall in love with the fuckee. The complementary motto might be: if your business is business, you don't fuck your business partner.

"Partner!" Alvaro bellowed when he saw me. "Partner! Steaks from Argentina!" He grabbed me around the neck with the arm that was holding a pronged barbeque fork and kissed me on the mouth. "One million down, nineteen million more to go! Tonight we party—hell, we party for nineteen more nights, right!" Then he squealed again and spun to the table behind the grill and poured me my own glass of tequila. I accepted the drink, and he raised his glass to mine but, before I could return the gesture, he had drained his glass and was pointing a finger at me, ominously. "Isn't there a way we can do it quicker? You know, move the money faster? I want to party nineteen more nights with you, but I want to do it knowing that all my money is safe."

I was a healthy man in his mid-thirties, and I believed that if I had to party nineteen nights in a row with Alvaro it would kill me. Or, if he spent them squealing and spinning and rambling as he had been all day, I would kill him before the first week was out.

I threw back my tequila before I spoke. "There are several reasons why it can't be done any more quickly, Alvaro. The main one is that the number of accounts we transfer into in the U.S. We have to keep those transfers under ten thousand to keep from raising any suspicion about what we are doing."

Alvaro poured himself another shot of tequila, drank it back, and hurled the barbeque fork across the patio.

I would have loved to have it all done too—if only because of Alvaro's bizarre behavior—and I had put the bug in Jack's ear about speeding things up, but as it stood the circumstances called for patience.

"Did you tell your friend Jack what will happen to him if they fuck my account up and lose my money?"

I sighed, but softly, so Alvaro wouldn't pick up on my frustration. "There was no need to say anything, Alvaro. These are honest people we're dealing with."

Alvaro made a sound like a squirrel on meth. I was loving the ride—high flying among the possibilities: becoming an almost-overnight millionaire, getting caught and landing in jail, the U.S. government seizing Citizen's National and guaranteeing only two hundred and fifty-thousand dollars for each depositor, slicing my stake in this operation to a sliver and putting me on the wrong side of a kingpin; it was Alvaro's apparent and unhinged joy with our progress that was unnerving me. I couldn't figure out if he was truly coming mentally unhinged, or if he was simply going to relish making my life miserable until the day this deal was done. But, when you're at a loss for how to reply to an over-stimulated woodland creature, change the subject: "Where are your wife and kids tonight, Alvaro? I was thinking on my way over I'd get to see your kids, and finally meet your—"

"Why do you care, Clint?" he asked, grinning like the maniac he either was or was pretending to be for the evening, then suddenly shouting, "Hey, I'm hot as hell!" and taking a running leap into the deep end of the pool.

The wave he created splashed over me, dampening my shirt and soaking me from the knees down. Alvaro surfaced and saw me looking with disdain at my wet pants. "Ha, ha, ha! Now you have no reason not to take off your clothes and come in, too! Aren't you hot, Clint, my partner? Doesn't the water feel good? My wife has taken the boys to her mother's and won't be back until morning, so take off your pants! Let me see what kind of underwear you have on under there! Bet you wear Calvin's, don't you? Come on in!"

Oh, boy, I groaned, but silently; *here it comes.* Time for me to bed down my business partner and he's never going to take no for an answer, not in the state he's in right now— There had been a time in my life when trading sex for whatever it was I needed or wanted in the moment had not felt like any big deal. But I had grown up. Or, maybe it wasn't merely age, maybe it had been falling in love that had done it; maybe it had been Taavi who had made me see that sex could actually mean something between two people that soared above the physical. Made me want to continue to soar instead of just reverting once more to rutting.

And then I noticed smoke billowing from the direction of the grill, two hundred bucks of prime Argentinian beef about to go up in flames, and I grabbed a pair of tongs resting on the stainless steel lip to flip them off the heat and onto an Uayma platter on the table behind the grill.

Alvaro, whooping, hoisted himself up on the side of the pool. "Good catch, my friend!" he cheered, whooping again and clapping wildly as he crossed the patio to pick up one of the thick white towels folded on one of the lounge chairs, stopping only to vigorously towel himself dry. "Good catch—you saved our dinner, my partner!"

I watched him throw the towel over his head to sponge the water out of his thick, dark hair. For a moment I thought the distraction of the grill fire had saved me, that he was completely distracted again and the only things that would have to get wet that night were my ankles, but Alvaro romped across the patio to grab my hand.

"Come, my partner! There is a reason my wife isn't home tonight—I have a surprise for you!" he said and yanked me toward the table where the steaks were still sizzling on their platter.

I could feel my heart sinking in my chest, but I knew better than to reject him. And to get through it I would have to conjure a fantasy greater than any I'd ever let myself dream in the past. I let him drag me to the table and push me into one of the cushioned chairs.

"Here we are, here is your surprise," he continued, picking up the iPhone that was resting near the platter on the tabletop. His fingers moved quickly, pressing and swiping, until he found the screen he was looking for. "Here, my friend. Have a look for yourself."

I directed my eyes to the screen, unsure if I should be relieved that he seemed once again distracted or bracing myself for worse to come. What he wanted to show me were pictures of men. Nude men, men in their underwear, fully clothed men, young men, older men, pictures from the front, pictures from the back, pictures from the side, candid photos of men with crew cuts, studio portraits of men with locks Hollywood starlets would envy, snapshots of bald men at the very grill from which I'd just saved the steaks, average men, ugly men, stunningly beautiful men—Alvaro swiped through the photographs at a dizzying pace, grunting at each new face as if he was punctuating the view. He'd swiped through thirty, maybe forty photographs before he slapped the phone back on the table and asked me if I knew why he was showing me the faces of all of these men.

I swallowed. "Not really, Alvaro."

Alvaro laughed, but ruefully, no longer the child on a sugar high, once again the dark, ruthless man with whom I was comfortable. "I'm showing you these faces because they all belong to men I was associated with at one time. All of them let me down in one way or the other. Some of them revealed information they should have considered private, some stole from me. I considered most of them friends—the ones that stole from me would have only had to ask and I would have gladly given them whatever they wanted. When I make a friend I expect loyalty in all matters. When that trust is violated"—Alvaro shrugged, and sighed—"I have to retaliate in the only way I know."

I nodded my head in understanding, keeping eye contact, not blinking. "I understand what you're saying." I placed a hand on his knee and moved my face closer to his. "I don't like it either, when someone is disloyal to me. I promise you that if I ever have a problem with you I will tell you directly. I expect the same from you."

Before he could answer me, the outside security lights blazed on, and sounds of doors opening and closing came from the main house. His kids darted out of the house, toward us. Alvaro looked alarmed but, as the kids ran to him, he deftly flipped the phone so that it faced the table, the photographs hidden from his children, and he stooped and held out his arms so they could run into them. "My sons! What are you doing home? You are supposed to be at your abuela's house with your mother!"

The boys giggled as their father kissed their necks. "Javi peed in his pants!" Alvaro, Junior tattled.

"No!" Javi complained, "Mami said we didn't have to tell Papa!"

"Papa knows you're just a baby!" Alvaro,

Junior taunted and, as Javi began to wail in protest, Alvaro scooped them up in his arms and started toward the house. "Sofia! Sofia," he called as he moved inside, "what are you doing home? I told you I had business tonight and to go to your mother's—"

"What was I supposed to do? He peed in his pants, all over my mother's good sofa—"

"He is a baby!"—to which Javi responded by redoubling the efforts of his wails—"you could not think to take extra clothing for your baby son—"

That was as far as the domestic disagreement had progressed before I made it to the other side of the patio and slipped quietly out to the driveway and into my car.

My cell phone rang as I drove the long stretch of highway from the hacienda, back into Mérida. I drove in silence, my hands still shaking slightly, the aftereffect of seeing Alvaro's portrait gallery, that jolt of pure, delectable adrenaline.

"Hello, Jack."

"Hey, Clint. Quite a day we've had."

I chuckled but so softly Jack didn't hear. "You could say."

"Hey, Clint, I've got to tell you something that's bugging me."

"OK."

"Well, Alvaro..."

"Yeah?"

"He called me thirteen times at the office today, you know, to find out how the transfers were coming along, but that was all over hours ago and he keeps calling this evening and—"

"Yes?"

"He seems a little... He seems a little fucking bonkers, you know?"

The last thing I needed was one of my partners thinking—knowing?—that the other one was crazy. "He's just happy, and excited, Jack. He's gregarious, you know, by nature—"

"Sure, sure, Clint, but, here's the thing..."

"What?"

"How did he get my cell number?"

Apparently mine wasn't the only life Alvaro was going to make miserable until this whole business was over with.

20

JACK CONVINCED ME to talk to his parents. "Look, my dad's had business partners up his ass all his life. Board members, investors—if anyone can tell you how to handle Alvaro, it's him."

"Yes, but were any of them certifiably insane?" I regretted telling Jack about the show Alvaro had put on at his hacienda earlier in the evening and hyperbole—or, what I hoped was gross overstatement, in any case—seemed the only way to soften the blow.

"Just talk to Dad."

And so, the very next day I did. I was stretched out on a lounge chair on my patio, nursing a beer after a successful Day Two of transferring another million into the U.S., entirely exhausted, not from honest labor—because the only labor involved in my project was hauling bags of money out of Alvaro's hacienda and into the bank, and the bank's employees did that—and not from the stress that nearly always accompanies the rousing stimulation of doing something that's forbidden and getting away with it. No, my exhaustion came from fielding yet another day of Alvaro's incessant, increasingly demanding phone calls. "Is my money safe?" "How much is transferred now?" "When do I see a statement from your bank?" "*I don't give a fuck if you gave me a receipt from those armored car people, you're fucking taking my money out of my country and I don't know where it is so I can use it!*"

Jack and David and Candace were on the other end of the telephone call, huddled around the island in David and Candace's kitchen, Jack's cell phone on speaker so we could all talk together. I could hear ice clinking as David rolled cubes around in his glass of single malt, and I could almost see Candace rolling her eyes.

"It seems to me the simplest answer is to invite Alvaro to come to Miami and take him to the bank so he can see where his money is," Candace said, the voice of reason.

"Except that I don't want him to have simple answers," I told her. "I mean, I don't want him to see how easy it is on our end to move his money—if he does, he might decide he doesn't need us as middle men, which means I don't get my cut, and I don't get to buy a share of the bank, and, hell, it might mean that he takes his business to another bank entirely—"

"That would require him to find another bank—and other bankers—to take it to, explain to them how you're doing it, and convince them to buy in," Candace said evenly. "And, you've admitted, you don't think he's capable of that."

I nodded and then added, "I still don't think that." Because, obviously, she couldn't hear my head rattle.

"So we don't let him see how straightforward the transfers are." David rolled his ice around in his glass again; even separated by several hundred miles I could hear him thinking. "I take him to the bank, give him a tour—get him to sign a signature card so he feels official and introduce him to a few of the officers so he feels important. Take him into my office and offer him a drink—walk him through a few of the subtler details of the transactions, you know, that each nine-thousand-and-nine-hundred-dollar deposit remains in any dormant account for a matter of only minutes before it's transferred out again, and how we circumnavigate the problem of monthly statements so some nosey relative doesn't inadvertently come into possession of an aging parent's bank documents and get suspicious. I've talked my way through enough investor meetings in enough board rooms over the years, Clint, trust me, I can make trading Pokemon cards sound like the most complicated financial transaction in the known world if I have to."

I suppressed a laugh, though I distinctly heard Jack giggle out loud—probably because he was as surprised as I was that David even knew what Pokemon cards were.

"David, you'll need to be careful about which officers you introduce him to—if he finds out that the FDIC has the bank on its watch list, and that there's a limit of two hundred-and-fifty thou in insurance on any single account, man, that's a whole new level of paranoia we'll be dealing with—"

"Clint, do you honestly think an officer of the bank is going to announce the bank's problems to someone I introduce as a new customer? Who's being paranoid now?"

"Yeah, well, maybe so, David, but you haven't been down here dealing with a lunatic for two days—with eighteen more to go." I took a swig of my beer. "And let's not mention anything about me using part of my cut to buy an interest in the bank either. I can't think of a reason on earth why Alvaro would need to know that."

"Neither can I, Clint," David agreed.

"So"—I heard Candace tap the top of the kitchen counter with a ringed finger, gold clinking on marble—"we're decided. Tomorrow's Friday—Clint, you put Alvaro on his plane to Homestead. Jack will pick him up and bring him to the house—the first order of business will be a nice family luncheon, let him feel as if he's getting to know us as well as the bank."

"Nice touch, Mom—"

"Just give Jack a call in the morning and tell him what time he'll be landing."

I nodded, more to myself than for their benefit, of course. "One major obstacle. Not that I think Abe would just show up at your house unannounced"—I hesitated, trying to be delicate in my wording—"I know you're not all best friends right at the moment, but there's always the possibility, and then, what about running into him when you take Alvaro to the bank—"

"Got it covered"—Jack interrupted me—"there's a Rotary Club lunch tomorrow in Miami. They asked me a month ago to be the guest speaker—funding options for start-ups or something—I just didn't want to do it so I bowed out and they had to book a biologist who's doing research on pythons overtaking the Everglades. I'll call my buddy who invited me in the first place, get him to bump the biologist and send Abe down there to give the talk they really wanted. There's no way he'll pass up the opportunity to be the big shot and, between the time it takes to drive there and the luncheon itself, we can count on Abe being out of the picture for a good three hours. By the time he gets back I'll either be driving Alvaro back to the airport or have talked him into staying the night and hitting the gay bars in South Beach where, we all know, Abe would never be caught dead."

"My little genius," Candace said. I could almost hear her smile. "Now, hang up, fellas, so I can start to plan the menu for this momentous gathering."

I clicked off my phone and drained my beer and then wandered into my bedroom. I clicked on the TV, stripped off my shirt and lounged on the bed, not quite ready for sleep. I thumbed through an article in *Fortune* about preparing for retirement; based on their formula it would take a person thirty years to accumulate four million dollars, if that person had a cool one million to invest upfront. *Suckas*, I said out loud, and grinned. On TV a reporter was voicing over a video of a young hoodlum being escorted into jail—"This latest arrest is more evidence that our country is winning the war on drugs."

"Yeah, right," I talked back to her, "if you think any country's winning the war on drugs, *you're* on drugs."

21

AT SEVEN THE next morning my phone buzzed. "We've got a busy day today, my friend," Alvaro said, "get your ass out of bed and get ready to transfer my monies."

I hit mute, so he wouldn't hear me sigh. Then: "I'll be ready in twenty minutes."

"I'm leaving at nine to head to Homestead, so get over here and watch your armored car take away my money. I want my receipt before I leave."

I stood over the toilet trying to pee softly while I talked. "That's the plan, Alvaro."

"My wife told me she wished you'd stayed longer the other night. She hoped you didn't leave because of her or the kids."

Of course I left because of her and the kids, and he knew that. "No, no, I just wanted to get home and be rested to start work again in the morning. There will be plenty of time for family and fun in a few weeks, when all of our business is done. Don't you agree?" I used one hand to slide my speedo on and headed down the stairs to my pool.

"Oh, yes, my friend, there will be plenty of time for my family and you to know each other. Plenty of time!"

I clicked off the phone, laid it on a poolside table and dove in the chilly water. For my money—and there would soon be plenty of that too—a cold swim in the morning was more invigorating than caffeine. I put in my standard twenty laps in the water, and did a hundred crunches poolside, before I stretched out on a lounger to drink a quick cup of coffee and enjoy the pastry Pedro brought me. Even taking my time to scan through the daily newspapers, I was showered, shaved, dressed for another day of money exchanging, and on my way to Alvaro's by eight AM sharp.

Once again, the transportation of the money from the hacienda to the bank went seamlessly, aside from Alvaro getting in the way, his shouted commands ping-ponging between paranoia and vanity—"This is my money, Clint, my partner, and today I am going to go visit it where you put it in the United States bank and your friends better show me it is right where you said it is going to be," and "Clint, my friend, come here and tell me if you like this shirt or another one for me—I am meeting all my American partners today and I want to impress them and look my best!"

Once again, the transfer of the money into the U.S. accounts worked flawlessly. I sat in Juan Carlos's office, rather mesmerized by the blinking green digits on the computer screens, watching the familiar names associated with each account scroll by, wondering what their owners were doing at this very moment—being offered their morning meds by a cheerful LPN? Having a sheet drawn over their no longer breathing bodies by a sullen orderly, in preparation for being wheeled down the nursing home hall and out of this world? I was supposedly supervising the transfers but, really, all there was for me to do was to total in my head the growing amount of cash fattening my personal bank account with each new deposit, and field Alvaro's increasingly demanding calls to my cell—"How are the transfers coming along? How much is in my account now?" and "And now how much?" and "And now, you are keeping track of how much is in my account now?" The calls didn't stop until nearly eleven-thirty AM, when his plane landed in Homestead and Jack picked him up at the airport and, mercifully, took him off my hands for a few hours.

Once again I was annoyed and emotionally exhausted at the end of what was, in all reality, and especially when you tallied the earnings, a pretty damned easy workday. I had had intentions, when I left the bank, of stopping by the school I was building to check on how the construction was coming along—I hadn't shown my face there since before I'd met Alvaro and our scheme got underway—but if there was a problem to be solved on site I was in no frame of mind to handle its solution. I thought about just heading home, asking Pedro to make me a simple lunch and spending the day lounging by the pool, but I knew myself too well to think that would be relaxing—I would spend the entire time brooding about what was happening in Miami, wondering how David and Candace and Jack were coping with our unstable business partner, fearing that someone up there would drop the wrong sort of information to Alvaro and, rather than reassuring him, his little sojourn north would serve only to fuel his increasingly obsessive distrust. In the end I drove myself to the Teatro Armando Manzanero, where there was a special preview performance of the Symphony Orchestra of Yucatan that afternoon. They were presenting Dvorak's Concerto for Violin and I thought that a visit to the Czech Republic might be a fitting diversion, dispel my menacing mood until Jack called me this evening to tell me how he and his parents had fared through Alvaro's visit. As soon as I'd taken my seat in the theater I had the disquieting thought that Alvaro might really take Jack up on his offer to go partying in South Beach that night, the mayhem and miscommunication that might result in a drunken Alvaro trying to get information out of—or, Christ, *threatening*—an equally libated Jack, but the first movement had started. I turned off my cell phone and let these fearful thoughts be carried away, at least for a few hours, by the strings.

"Mom says that Alvaro's six-pack is 'delicious'," Jack laughed. "I mean, man, he really is good looking. It's a shame he's such a dick..."

I had taken it as a very good sign that, emerging from the symphony more relaxed and refreshed than I'd felt in days, there were no frantic voice mails waiting for me from Alvaro when I turned my cell phone back on. This call from Jack served to blow away any lingering residue of anxiety.

"He and Dad talked bullfighting—Alvaro insisted on Dad calling Chester so he could meet him in person. He treated Chester like a goddamn celebrity, 'my own, personal connection to the great Ernesto Pastor', he told him. Charming as all hell."

"And Abe?" I asked, needing to be sure that his trip to the Miami Rotary had gone off without a hitch and he and Alvaro hadn't come within the thirty-five miles between Homestead and Miami of each other.

"Oh, well, get this, guess who Abe ran into at Rotary?"

"Who?" Good news never comes when someone asks you to 'guess who'. I could feel my gut tighten, the effects of the soothing violins being squeezed out of me.

"An old friend of yours," he teased.

"Jack, for fuck's sake, tell me who you're talking about!"

"Xavier Sousa."

22

WHEN JACK AND I were in our freshman year at college, I'd made a deal with one of my finance professors, a certain cretin called Brad Goldstein—a deal that, if you weren't being generous, you could call a bribe. I really wanted an 'A' in his class, as opposed to the 'B' I was in line to get—I was a kid, just eighteen, and I didn't think I could bear facing David with less than a stellar grade in such a core subject—and Brad really wanted to suck my cock. One afternoon after class, instead of walking away down the hall when I noticed him staring again at the zipper in my jeans, I approached him. "What's it going to take to boost my final grade up a letter?" I'd asked. Brad locked the classroom door and got down on his knees.

I'd leveraged my good looks before—a high school teacher or coach or guidance counselor who needed an extra incentive to go the extra mile on my behalf—but it wasn't until I was eighteen and met Brad that I realized the full extent of the power I possessed simply because I was young and beautiful. Brad seemed to think our little tussle on the teacher's desk that day meant that we were now in some sort of a relationship; thankfully our grades had already been posted before he became insistent about it and it was a simple matter of telling him that if he didn't back off I would report him to the dean for molesting a student. I thought I had the world by the ass.

Then I met Xavier Sousa, lead counsel for Zimmerman, Black, and Sousa, ostensibly a happily married father of five, handsome, rich, connected, absolutely aglow with confidence. I was young enough to respect a man who had, for ten years in a row, been named the top lawyer in Miami by the *Miami Herald* for no other reason than that he had the kind of wealth and position I craved for myself; I was naïve enough to think that what I brought to the table—a pretty face attached to a willing, rock hard cock—would make him want to protect me at all costs.

I was also, at the time, confused about my sexuality. I had girlfriends a plenty, but I never passed up an opportunity to be with a man either; I don't think I'd ever heard the term 'bisexual' before in my life, and I thought there was no end to what Xavier could teach me about that part of myself.

He paid off my student loans and, for the first and only time in my life, I gave over my power to someone else—and I did it willingly, because my affection for Xavier Sousa was as disconcertingly real as someone who'd never before in his life experienced a romance could imagine.

At first, there was no question the exchange was working in my favor. Xavier set me up in a one-bedroom apartment in a new condo development overlooking Biscayne Bay. I'd always been a careful dresser, but I'd never shopped at Versace or Cartier, not on my student budget, and Xavier took me to those places—and always treated when we got to the cash register. In Miami he and I were business associates, mentor and mentee or, if the occasion called for it, doting uncle and attentive nephew; on the trips he arranged in Italy and France and Switzerland, he introduced me as his lover and, while I bristled at the possession the term implied, I also enjoyed the freedom of being able to claim it. He got me my first financial consulting job at Merrill Lynch, and was so successful at cajoling his rich friends into using me to make their investments that within my first year

I was managing fifty million in investment accounts.

The arrangement worked for nearly five years. Xavier kept me on a fairly tight leash, but I didn't really mind since the sex was always pretty great, and because I knew he was the one who'd enabled me to have such a quick rise in the business world. But a man changes in the years between twenty-one and twenty-six. I'd acquired my own set of clients entirely separate from the ones Xavier had sent to me when I was just starting out. I was the top producer at Merrill in my last three years there—because I didn't sit back and do the traditional investments, funds and stocks. Instead, I set up limited real estate partnerships for my wealthiest clients, and I did it with no debt, saving a ton of money. In eighteen months, I would flip the partnership and double everyone's money—including mine. In that same time, I matured into my own set of opinions, preferences, desires, and there wasn't a lot of room for those things in Xavier's world. I wanted to go back to Amsterdam on our next vacation and Xavier wanted to take a cruise ship along the Alaskan coast; we'd ended up among the glaciers. I wanted to stay at home, order in pizza, pop some brews, and watch the Dolphins and Xavier wanted to go out and try that new French restaurant; I ended up eating escargot. I wanted to fuck and Xavier wanted to sleep, so we ended up in a huge fight before I went to the bathroom to jack off. Such, I can suppose in retrospect, were the dangers of any relationship with the sort of age difference that separated Xavier and me.

The end of the relationship came suddenly, the night he caught me in bed with a young woman I'd met at Merrill. Monica and I had been fucking all night. She and I were laying in my bed, watching the sun come up over Biscayne Bay, used condoms strewn across the floor like dust bunnies, and we were both stunned when Xavier walked into the bedroom as though he owned it. I jumped out of the bed and hustled Xavier into the kitchen without bothering to put on any clothes.

"Jesus, Xavier, what the fuck?" I whispered, trying to be discreet so Monica wouldn't be alarmed.

Xavier didn't return the favor. "I own that," he shouted, grabbing at my cock that was still semi-hard from my late exertions.

I batted his hand away. "What? Are you jealous? You've got a wife, what the hell are *you* jealous about?" I backed away from him. In truth, I'd always liked the fact that he had a family life separate from me; it kept him from holding the leash he had around me too tightly for me to breathe. I also enjoyed how being with Xavier kept my life from getting too complicated—knowing I had to answer to him allowed me to keep my distance with the many women I slept with.

Xavier put his head in his hands, ashamed of himself, I guessed. "I love you," he mumbled into his fingers.

"Oh, shit, Xavier."

That morning, before the sun had completely risen, I'd moved out of the condo Xavier had bought for me and into a hotel until I could find and close on a place of my own.

"Did you ever love Xavier?" Jack asked.

I shrugged. "I liked him, I respected him. I was in awe of him, I think. And, yah, I did care about him, but more like I would a father..."

Jack laughed. "I never wanted to have sex with my father."

"He represented a *father figure* to me, you idiot."

There was silence on the other end of the line. I glanced out the window as I continued. "To be totally honest with you, I'm ashamed of my behavior with him. Xavier wasn't a saint, mind you, but he always wanted more from me than I was willing to give and I went along with it—led him on, I think. I wanted to live in his world so badly back then that I was willing to do anything to get inside."

Still, silence from Jack.

"Jack? What? What else?"

"You think you could work with him again?"

"Why do you ask?"

"Because when Abe ran into him at Rotary he told him the bank was open to investors and Xavier said he was interested. He and Dad and Abe have a meeting Monday morning."

23

S UNDAY MORNING. A quick swim, some crunches, a leisurely breakfast over the newspapers, a drive to walk around the school I was building. The construction crew wouldn't be there on a Sunday, but I could check on the progress they were making and talk to Miguel, the architect, on Monday morning about any issues I discovered that needed attention. I'd been meaning to waylay Miguel in any case. His brother, Pablo, also had a connection to a drug cartel—the same one as Alvaro or a different one, I had no idea—and I wanted to see if I could wring some more information from him about how the cartels operated. I had met Pablo once, actually, years before, when I was in the midst of restoring my house. I'd hired Miguel as my architect, and he and I hadn't seen eye-to-eye on either the quality of the work he was doing or how non-efficiently he was meeting my deadlines—so I'd fired him.

Miguel threatened, "If you don't allow me to finish this project my brother will send your ass back to the U.S. in a box!" He'd stormed out of what were then the ruins of my house, and then stormed back a few hours later with his brother, Pablo, in tow.

I was—frankly, and probably less secretly than I would have liked—terrified that a cartel boss was standing in my house. All I knew about such men at the time was what I read in American newspapers and, accordingly, what I had been expecting was some crude, foul-mouthed, ill-educated thug arriving to shake me down in an effort to preserve his brother's honor. I had, actually, contemplated not being home when Miguel returned with his sibling, and would not have been except that my curiosity got the better of my fear. That didn't mean I wasn't shaking when I opened the door to Miguel's insistent knocking.

"I am Pablo Navarro," Pablo had said by way of introduction, a white linen blazer draped over broad shoulders, calm and stately in his speech while Miguel stood behind him, his lips in the sort of pout I supposed had once probably impressed his mother but that, truly, he should have grown out of at his age. "Show me what you are so upset with my little brother about, please, Señor Kennedy."

So Pablo and I had walked around my house, outside and in, over piles of broken tiles, through sawdust, picking our way around random tools left to scratch the hardwood floors and a dead bird left to rot on my patio.

Pablo took it all in, then turned to his brother and said, "You have always been lazy, Miguel, haven't you?" To me he said, "Please, as a favor to me, Señor Kennedy, let my brother finish the job. I will make sure he shows up on time, and that he does the most beautiful work in all of Mérida." He turned back to his brother. "You are capable of beautiful work, Miguel. And that is what I want you to start doing *now*."

Miguel did as his brother had commanded, and more—I never again found the tiniest fault in his work. Moreover, Pablo and I seemed to have a connection, a mutual respect for work that was beautifully done, so there was even a chance I could meet again with the kingpin himself. I craved to know more about how the cartels worked, and it wasn't just the danger that was attractive—if Alvaro had twenty million in cash laying around, there must be others who had money in need of washing up, and why shouldn't I be their launderer as well?

Anyway, going to the site to check on the school was something productive to do to keep my mind off what could possibly transpire in a meeting between David and Xavier. It had been almost eight years, but was Xavier still pissed off at me? If he found out I was slated to be an investor in the bank, would he make an offer just to squeeze me out? David's affection for me ran deep, I knew, but could he be swayed by whatever Xavier would say if he decided to be vindictive? David certainly didn't know that Xavier and I had once been involved as more than merely mentor and mentee, and I was sure Xavier wouldn't want him to, but how vindictive was he willing to be?

I was nursing my third cup of Pedro's excellent coffee when my cell rang. Alvaro. A call I had been expecting though I debated sending it to voice mail because I didn't know what kind of stress he wanted to lay on me this morning, but I did know I couldn't handle much more of it. Not on a Sunday.

"Shit," I muttered, then punched the phone. "Hey, Alvaro, what's up?"

"Good morning, my friend! How are you this beautiful day? I want to take you on an adventure. I can pick you up in half an hour, can you be ready?"

I sighed. Well, at least he sounded as if he was in a good mood. "Sure," I told him.

I rode in the backseat of the Hummer, next to Alvaro, the driver and an extra thug in the front seat. We were on our way to what Alvaro described as his "retreat", a one-hour drive to the south. It was still early on a Sunday morning so the streets were clear—everybody else was either still asleep or in church. All Alvaro would tell me about our destination was that it was going to be a "big surprise" for me, a phrase that doesn't inspire confidence but does get the delicious adrenaline flowing.

The retreat looked like an old English castle dumped in the Mexican countryside. It had been built by a lonely old countess from East Sussex over one hundred years before. Alvaro kept a full-time staff for the tastefully elegant house and expansive grounds, though I clearly wasn't to get a tour of much more than the small stone outbuilding where the driver aimed the Hummer as soon as we entered under the estate's stone archway.

The thug who was riding shotgun that day got out of the car as soon as it was stopped and sprinted over to open a padlock on the building's thick wooden door. "Come," Alvaro said, waving his fingers at me and getting out of the car to follow the thug.

The outbuilding consisted of one room. Inside were over two hundred different firearms of various types—rifles, pistols, automatic machine guns. A couple of shoulder-fired rocket launchers.

"Today, I am going to teach you to shoot, my friend," Alvaro said, choosing two rifles, loading them easily with a steady, practiced hand, and shoving one of them into my hands.

I had never held a gun before in my life. The adrenaline that was coursing through my body made my legs feel hollow, but my hands weren't shaking.

I followed Alvaro as he walked to the back of his property where he had a firing range. The thug and the driver set up a target made of canvas with a painted white bulls-eye, stretched over bales of hay that would stop the bullets from going into the pasture where some of his cattle grazed.

"Zebu," he said, pointing at the livestock. "Mostly," he clarified while he lifted his rifle and sited the gun. "Some Charollais," he added, and fired. His bullet tore the canvas in the exact center of the target.

I couldn't have kept myself from jumping at the sound if I'd been warned it was going to happen, much to Alvaro's great amusement.

I wondered if that was how he got rid of people who disappointed him. Did he shoot and kill and then laugh at people who betrayed him?

"Come, get in front of me," he told me. I was reluctant to move and he sensed it. "You are worried about something, Clint? I am just going to stand behind you and give you advice so you shoot straight."

I moved to stand before him and lifted the gun to my shoulder as I'd seen him do. He planted a pair of ear protectors on my head so my own shot wouldn't startle me. Then he wrapped his arms around my body, and his hands around mine, gently positioning the gun at its target. "Pull the trigger when you are ready." I took a deep breath and flexed my finger.

My shot didn't come anywhere near any area of the target. "You will need much practice." Alvaro laughed, taking the gun from my hands and tossing it to the thug, who had already reloaded the gun Alvaro had been using and tossed that one to him in return. He lifted it to his shoulder and sighted the target once more but, instead of firing, he lowered the gun and turned to me.

"These are wonderful friends you have in Miami, Clint," he said.

I nodded. "I knew you'd like them. I've known them since I was a little boy. Jack and I grew up together."

"That's what David told me. I think you've put me in safe hands, Clint, my friend." He turned again to the target, lifting his gun. "I have only one question for you."

"Only one?" I forced myself to chuckle, removing the ear protectors from my head.

He turned to me with the rifle raised to his shoulder. "Why are you taking your money up front?" He held the gun on me. Sighting. "I think it would be better for you to wait until all the money is transferred and then you take the last bit for your fee." His body was so perfectly still it could have been a statue, the gun so relaxed in his hands, the barrel so squarely, solidly pointed at my chest. "Don't you think it would be better to do it that way too?"

I didn't know what I thought except that I was about to overdose on my favorite drug, adrenaline. I gripped the ear protectors to keep my hands—my whole body—from shaking so hard I'd shit my pants. I wanted to protest that I wasn't stealing from him. I had done a lot of questionable things in my life, but stealing wasn't one of them. I was merely taking the percentage he and I had agreed upon. What I said was, "Sure, Alvaro."

"Ah ha!" Alvaro laughed. "That will make me happy," he said as he spun toward the target again, fired, and tore a second hole in the canvas that kissed his first bull's-eye hit.

24

" **J** ACK." I'D DIALED him as soon as I saw Alvaro's Hummer pull away from the curb in front of my house. "We need to move the money faster."

The silence on the other end of the line made me realize how hard I was breathing. How strange I must sound.

"How fast do you mean, Clint?"

I made a conscious effort to get hold of my breathing. "How fast can you move?"

"Well"—I could almost hear Jack's gears start to move—"I actually had been thinking about what you and I already talked about— maybe we could do multiple transfers to the same accounts each day. Technically each wire is a separate transaction. The ten-thousand-dollar limit isn't about wires per se, but cash deposits."

"What would that translate to in terms of time?"

I could hear a beer cap popping on the other end. "It takes us about an hour to complete the transfer for one million. If we worked an eight-hour day, that means we could do eight million a day. There's seventeen million left that has to be transferred, so, conceivably, we work a little overtime and we could have it all done in two days."

"Do it. I'll make the arrangements on this end—"

Jack laughed. "Hold up a minute, Clint. I'll have to check with Dad, make sure he's got the Feds in hand and no one will be looking too closely at the bank while this is going on—and, even if Dad's on board, are you sure Juan Carlos can handle it?"

"You worry about your dad. I'll take care of Juan Carlos."

I popped a beer for myself while I waited for Jack to call me back with a yea or nay from David. If it was nay, well, I'd have to call David myself and have a conversation with him. I was damned if I was going to give Alvaro back a penny of the money I'd earned in the last few days; I needed this deal to be done before Alvaro had a chance to find that out.

I'd finished my beer and had started on another when my phone rang. "Jack?"

"No, Clint. It's David."

My hand froze with my bottle halfway to

my mouth. If David himself was calling this was either very good news, or very bad. "Yes, David."

"Yes."

"Yes, we can move the money tomorrow?"

"We can. I'll have to do some serious shuffling—I'll need to sideline Abe, for one thing. He sees that much new money coming in in one day and he'll know something's up and won't be happy."

"Can you do that?" It was almost painful to ask.

"There's a bank in West Palm that's about to be acquired by the Feds. I'll send Abe up there to look into acquiring it for us. That'll take at least a couple of days. By the time he gets back all the money will be transferred and he won't be able to do anything about it."

"But—"

"Won't he wonder why we're looking into acquiring another asset when we're about to lose our own shirts?"

"Yeah."

I could swear I heard him wink. "Money's fungible, Clint. Did you forget that?"

I took a long swallow of my beer. Damn, it tasted good.

"It occurs to me, too, Clint, that if all the money is transferred in the next two days, by tomorrow evening you'll have the full two million we agreed on for your purchase of stock."

I allowed myself a wide smile. "I will, David."

"Then it's time to arrange for the stock transfer. I'll have my lawyers draw up the papers. When can you get here to sign them?"

I thought. "I can fly up tomorrow after the transfers here are complete."

"And fly back tomorrow night so you're in Mexico again in time for Tuesday's business? That's an awfully ambitious schedule, Clint."

"We're closing an awfully big deal, David." I heard him chuckle. "I don't want any other investor edging me out," I added.

There was a pause on the other end of the line. "What are you talking about?"

I drained my bottle. What the hell? "I heard you have a meeting with Xavier Sousa tomorrow."

"Yes," David said slowly. "He's my attorney. Who do you think is going to draw up the papers for your stock transfer? Have— Have you been talking to Abe?"

"Jack." I felt like a heel for ratting him out.

"Both my sons are idiots."

Zimmerman, Black and Sousa. What were the chances that would be David's law firm,

I thought and, then, if I thought about it just a little harder, what were the chances it *wouldn't be*? Of course David would use the top firm in town for his business; I'd just never considered the connection before. I wondered if Xavier would be at the closing, and then I put that particular bit of curiosity aside—of course he would be there, if only to see me after all these years; the same reason I wanted him to be there. In spite of the messy end to our relationship, I was still grateful to him. For all my years of living amidst the Cohens, I hadn't really known my way around first class until I'd spent time with him and I would never be able to do enough to thank him for showing me around. And, as I sat on my patio, thinking about seeing him again, I realized I still wanted him to be proud of me, of what I had achieved. I wanted him, as much as I wanted David, to be proud of me, and to tell me so. I wanted to bask in their approval for being in the position to buy such a substantial share of Citizen's National Bank. I realized, somewhat to my amazement, that I missed Xavier.

It was a very unaccustomed feeling.

And I had no time for it at the moment. I had to call Alvaro to tell him I would be picking up eight million from him in the morning. And I had to call Juan Carlos to tell him to plan for a busy day. Alvaro would be pleased and suspicious, and Juan Carlos would be stunned, and possibly reluctant, but a reminder about the cut he was going to take for only two days' worth of work would, I was sure, be more than enough to incentivize him. Then I had to sit back and let it all sink in: within forty-eight hours I was going to be a multimillionaire—and a major stock holder in a soon-to-be prosperous bank.

If I had had a bottle of champagne in the house, I would have popped it. As it was, another bottle of Sol would have to suffice.

25

"THE MONEY IS already counted, so the bank's men have only to load it into their armored truck." I was due at Alvaro's hacienda at nine o'clock on Monday morning and I'd arrived at ten minutes to the hour. That he was ready to proceed early spoke to how eager he was as well for the transfers to be complete.

"Good. By tomorrow night this will all be over."

"And we will celebrate!" Alvaro cried. "But why wait? You will come here again when you're through at the bank this afternoon and we'll have some good Argentine steaks together at last, what do you say?"

"I say nothing would please me more, Alvaro, but I need to fly to Miami tonight."

He squinted at me, and I wondered if his good humor was now spent. "Why are you leaving tonight? We have another full day of work tomorrow to transfer the last of my money."

"Oh, I'll be back in plenty of time to over-see that—there's just some personal busi-ness I need to attend to in Florida. It won't take more than a few hours."

Alvaro considered his response. I took the very fact that my impetuous partner was being thoughtful as a good sign. "Do you know when we have finished this deal, I have another one waiting for you?"

I smiled—genuinely; I longed to know more about Alvaro's drug operation. So far he had been terribly secretive about it and would not tell me where he sourced his drugs, or what his distribution chain looked like. "If I tell you more, I must be first assured that you will make a life-long commitment to my business," he said to me, "and I am not sure you are ready for such a long-term rela-tionship. I hear that is not something you're good at—long-term relationships." Then he had laughed. "But I will tell you the money is much more than only twenty million!"

I longed to know how much more.

Good sense, however, told me to make good on my current promises to Alvaro and never make another one.

But just when, I wondered, had good sense ever been very attractive?

Four million dollars was more than enough for what I wanted in my life—something respectable and admirable, make my school the best it could be for those in need. Could I do that *and* continue to work with Alvaro?

"Alvaro," I said, "I think it's best if we conclude our current arrangement. When we're both satisfied with the results, we can talk about our next one."

Alvaro raised his eyebrows. "What business do you have in Miami tonight?"

I shrugged. "I'm seeing an old boyfriend."

This made him roar with laughter. "Then I will have my plane ready to take you to your rendezvous!"

"Thank you, Alvaro, that's really not necessary, I can go commercial—"

"Clint, my friend, I insist. Now! Go see Juan Carlos—I have a fight coming up on the weekend. Did you forget? While you're working I will be out killing a bull for practice!"

I hadn't forgotten about the fight. With all the activity around getting Alvaro's money and mine out of Mexico it hadn't been at the top of my mind, but it had occurred to me only the day before that it was yet another good reason to move the money out of Mexico at an accelerated pace—and to not obey

Alvaro's directive to put my share of it back in his account until all the transfers were complete; if something happened to Alvaro, either in practice for the fight or in the actual fight itself, I would be certain to have trouble in claiming what was mine. This way, *my* way, whether Alvaro lived or died, I won.

The transfer of the first large batch of wires—eight million dollars' worth—was tedious, if uneventful. Juan Carlos and I took a single break—for twenty minutes at around noon for a quick burrito and a beer—and by quarter to six that evening I was on my way to the hangar to take Alvaro's plane to Miami.

I asked Tim for a club soda with lime, which he went to fetch for me immediately, but I was clearly so preoccupied that he didn't even bother to flirt with me. I headed straight for the head, threw my duffle bag on the toilet lid, hung my garment bag on the door hook and unzipped it. Even with all the luxury of Alvaro's jet, this was cramped quarters for changing out of standard Mérida business attire—flax-colored linen shorts and a blue button-down shirt, sleeves rolled up—and into something more suitable for becoming a Miami bank owner. I'd chosen an ink blue Armani suit for the occasion, and I took my time with the pale blue silk tie I'd paired with it, going back and forth between a Windsor knot and a four-in-hand and finally opting for a Pratt.

In the cabin I sat on one of the long, white, leather sofas sipping my soda, thoughts of what I would do with my money circling in my brain. The school I was building for the Mayan kids was fully financed, as it was—two hundred thousand to open and another hundred to cover the first-year loss—but with my new wealth I could expand it. Maybe increase the number of children it could accommodate, add some classrooms and some teachers, develop more advanced curriculum. I smiled—it was the common understanding among educated and thoughtful people that the way you kept young people from falling into a life of drugs and desolation was to educate them, give them a solid shot at making a life for themselves that was better than the lives they saw around them, give them hope; the government wasn't doing that but, by God, I was waging my own personal war on drugs.

26

DAVID WAS AT the bottom of the stairs as I walked down with my backpack thrown over my shoulder. "Is that all you have, Clint?" he called up to me.

"This is it. I'll only be here this evening—I turn right around and go back as soon as we're done."

"Then let's get busy, my boy. We'll pick Candace up along our way. I would never have believed any of us would be so happy to sell part of the bank, but she might as well have been practicing her autograph all day, she's so eager to sign away."

"Have you heard anything out of Abe?" I threw my backpack into the back seat of the BMW and climbed inside, inhaling the rich scent of new leather.

"He knows nothing of our meeting today, and we're keeping it that way. He's far away in West Palm—"

"On a fool's errand?"

David shrugged. "Maybe, maybe not. That bank he's checking out would be a fine acquisition and, thanks to you, we'll soon have the wherewithal to actually acquire it. You've got a great way at getting to the bottom of things, Clint. I want you to take a look at the bank figures and tell me what you think. As your business in Mérida grows, we're going to need more locations."

David turned into his long driveway. Even from a distance I spotted Candace standing by the front door, pointing out to one of the gardeners exactly how she expected the climbing roses to be trimmed. She looked magnificent as usual: snow white linen slacks and crisp blazer, black heels, and, underneath, a sky-blue silk blouse that, I noticed, almost perfectly matched my beautifully tied tie. She turned when she heard David's car approach and lifted her arms in greeting.

David pulled up to the house and put the car in park, and I jumped out to hug Candace. "My young and handsome millionaire," she sang and took me in her arms.

The drive to downtown Miami was typical—bumper to bumper traffic, even at this hour of the evening. It was slow going with horns honking and impatient drivers swerving from one lane to another. It took us an hour and some change to reach Xavier's building—David driving with Candace beside him, me in the backseat but Candace turned as best she could, restricted by her seatbelt, to talk to me the whole way.

"You must be so happy to be seeing your mentor again," Candace said to me, and winked. I had always believed that she knew there was something more to my connection with Xavier than what we allowed the public to see, but she'd never said anything to me about it. She would think it was none of her business although, when Jack and I were in high school she had asked him once if we were boyfriends. "It's fine with me if you are, you know," she'd told her son. Jack, who was only lately, in his mid-thirties, growing out of his adolescent-asshole phase, had looked at her and replied, "Ah, Mom, Clint? I can do better than him."

"I am excited to be seeing Xavier again. He was a terrific role model for me when I was younger—I've never gone wrong following his advice."

David tapped his horn, not to join the general cacophony of the heavy traffic, but in agreement with my sentiment. "You have always made the most of every opportunity offered to you, Clint. Candace and I are so proud of you!" He shook his head. "We had high hopes for all our boys..."

When we pulled up to Xavier's building, his personal valet met us and signaled us to pull tight to the sidewalk so he could relieve us of David's car. One of Xavier's private secretaries was waiting for us as we entered the building. "Right this way, Mr. and Mrs. Cohen, Mr. Kennedy."

Xavier had purchased the building for a song just the year before, when the whole real estate market was just starting to go to shit. Xavier never knew it, but one of the limited partnerships I had set up at Merrill owned that building. Investors had wanted to cash out, so I'd told the broker to contact Xavier and make it happen. It was a twenty-four-story, wanna-be Art Deco building, constructed in the late 1990s, but with attention to quality materials and authentic detail. The lobby featured a two-story white-and-cream-and-ecru-and-beige mural that you could see was composed of a variety of sea creatures found along Florida's coast, if you looked hard enough, and white marble floors that made each footfall echo in the large open space, all encased in a glass façade. Every space in the building was rented at any given time—the top two floors housed Xavier's law firm and, so, this was downtown's status address.

The secretary escorted us to the board

room on the twenty-third floor, where Xavier waited. He locked eyes on me as we entered, and walked to me. I offered my hand and he took it in both of his. He was as handsome as he ever was, I thought, and was surprised when he leaned in and whispered, "You look as good today as you always did," at the same moment. Had we always thought in concert like this, I wondered, and answered myself: Yes.

Xavier turned to David and Candace and shook hands with them as well. Then he waved his hand toward the array of legal documents laid out on the table before us. "You do realize that after you sign these documents, David, you and Candace will no longer have primary control of the bank?"

Candace tilted her head. "If we don't sign these documents there won't be any bank to control, Xavier." David remained silent, and I was sure the reason was that, though I was buying half of their collective shares, he was sure I would still defer to him concerning operations—and he wasn't entirely wrong about that. I had no interest in spending my days in a bank office, or living my life exclusively in Miami, and he knew it.

"And the funds for this purchase?" Xavier asked. "They've been transferred?"

"Clint has seen to that."

Xavier raised his eyebrows. In the arch of his eyes I saw the question: *where did Clint get two million dollars to buy a bank?* In the smile that played on his lips, I read both pride and amusement that, however it had been accomplished, I had pulled it off.

With a few flourishes of black ink—first David's, then Candace's, then mine—I was the owner of a thirty-two-percent stake in Citizen's National Bank, equal to David and Candace's shares combined; the remaining thirty-eight percent of stock was owned by approximately eighty individual owners. As the ink dried, each of us sat back in our chairs, speechless—each for a different reason—at the magnitude of what we had just done.

"I think," Xavier broke the silence, "that this calls for a little celebration. May I take you all to dinner? I own a very nice restaurant, one flight up."

Xavier had invested in the top-floor restaurant so that he could have the convenience of entertaining clients and friends in his own building. The maître d' straightened his striped bow tie as we entered and, I could have sworn, nearly tapped his heels together to signal his attention.

"I'll be four this evening, Charles," he told him.

"Very good, Mr. Sousa," the maître d' replied and led us through the broad, open, modern space with floor-to-ceiling windows offering an unparalleled view of Biscayne Bay, to the back of the restaurant where he parted a heavy white linen curtain onto a sizeable but still cozy nook that held Xavier's private table. The round, cherry wood table was set for six as we entered; four waiters followed close on our heels, two to strip the table of two of its place settings and rearrange the charger plates, silver utensils, and soft linen napkins that had been folded into the shapes of swans for our smaller party, and two to hold our chairs and seat us—Candace first, of course, then David, then me, and Xavier last. The waiters were all young men in their early twenties, all striking to look at, and, though they seemed terribly efficient about their jobs, I wondered how many of them had been hired because in addition to their skills they were amazing eye candy for Xavier.

"The wine list, Mr. Sousa, or would you prefer to start with cocktails?" Charles asked.

"Candace?" Xavier asked. "I defer to your better judgment."

"I wouldn't turn down a vodka martini. Straight up. Dry."

"All around?" Xavier held up a hand as

if he was going to do a head count. When no one objected to his suggestion he said, "Four Tovaritch martinis, Charles."

"Yes, indeed, Mr. Sousa. Right away."

The four of us talked banking over our martinis, then our flakey, succulent appetizers, beggar's purses stuffed with crab and served with a Loire Valley Pouilly Fumé, our steak au poivre accompanied by a rich, peppery Côtes du Rhône—"I'm so old school when it comes to good food," Xavier had offered as if it were a confession, though I knew his tastes to be a point of pride. He had ordered for the table, at our request; it was his restaurant, after all, and who better to know the true specialties of the house? I enjoyed the meal, but I couldn't help flashing back to my years with Xavier, all the French food I'd ingested, even when I would have preferred pizza or a burger, because it was Xavier's favorite cuisine.

"So, you believe the loan department needs to be remade?" David asked me.

"From top to bottom," I confirmed after swallowing a bite of my steak. "Look, some of the bad loans Abe made might have to be written off, but how many more might be salvageable? Why wouldn't we consider modifying the payments to help bring the borrowers current rather than throwing up our hands and scrapping the whole she-bang? It's good for us if we recover our money, even eventually, and it's good for the customers and their credit ratings, in the end, too. Seems to me that's much more of a win-win outcome."

"I agree," Candace offered. "Let's bring in someone to look over what's on the books and rate the loans as far as collectability and see what we can work out with the customers."

"I have someone in mind who would be very helpful with that," I said.

David nodded. "Give me his contact information. I'll call him in for an interview."

"Of course. But, David, it's a *her*," I told him, and Candace giggled.

"Sexist pig," she said, smiling at her husband.

David laughed at himself. "Busted. Any other bright ideas, Clint?"

"Well, I'd like to talk about two of our board members who are over eighty years old. They don't understand modern banking and I think it's time for them to go. Also, of course, we need to up the deposits, which should make the FDIC very happy—more money coming in than going out." I stole a glance at Xavier, who had been quietly observing while he ate his meal, not speaking much at all, preferring to assess the deal he had just facilitated, the fiscal health of the bank, and the current status of my life from what he could glean from our conversation. "My partner in Mexico," I said, purposely leaving out what kind of partner I was talking about, to keep Xavier guessing, "is working on another venture for the two of us, one that could be worth five times the one we've just completed"—I paused while David dabbed his mouth with his napkin, to cover his gasp—"and I'm certain he'll bring the business to us."

David smiled broadly, and Candace raised her glass of Côtes du Rhône to me, and I saw Xavier grin. "Quite a good partner to have, I'd say," Xavier offered.

"Oh, yes, he is," I replied. And then I felt good for exactly twenty seconds, until I realized that bringing in more of Alvaro's money to the bank meant I'd have to continue to deal with Alvaro himself. My brain was suddenly awash in clichés—caught between a rock and a hard place; choose between the devil and the deep blue sea; in for a penny, in for a pound—and I absolutely could *not* give any sign of being even slightly shaken because there, to my immediate left, was Xavier, taking it all in. Suddenly, and without even a wink to David or Candace in consultation, these words were out of my mouth: "I would also love to talk with you, Xavier, about being on our board of directors. It would certainly be to our advantage to have the best lawyer in the state on the inside."

To my relief, and after only the briefest moment of stunned silence, David and Candace enthusiastically, and in unison, seconded my motion.

Xavier smiled at me. "I will certainly consider it, then, Clint." I held out my hand to him for a handshake, and once again he took it in both of his and held it while he continued. "I wouldn't mind at all having an excuse to spend more time with you again."

My phone buzzed as we were in the car, David and Candace driving me back to the airport.

Alvaro.

"How was your practice today?" I greeted him.

"Ah! It was not good. The bull trapped me behind a barrel and I had to have one of my guys chase him off. This bull is crazy! Crazier than any I've ever seen, and big! But you wait and see, when I am through with him he will be meat on the grill!" Well, he was in a good mood.

"Alvaro," I said, because clearly either becoming an over-night millionaire, or the proximity to my old mentor, or the vodka had gone to my head and I, myself, was in the mood for brash, rash decisions, "what do you think of me inviting David and Candace to come to Mexico this weekend to see you fight?"

The response from all three parties—the one on the phone and the two in the front seat of the car—was immediate: "Of course, invite them!" and "Couldn't imagine a better offer, my genius boy!" and "That's a lovely idea, dear."

When I was settled back into the lush sofa on Alvaro's plane, and Tim had served me a small glass of brandy, my phone rang again. Jack this time.

"Your mom and dad are coming to visit me in Mexico this weekend."

"Huh," Jack grunted. "So, you didn't think Mom and Dad selling you half their shares in the bank was quite enough to piss Abe off," he deadpanned.

"You know, Jack," I confessed, "and nothing at all to do with the reason I asked your parents to come visit me, but I really do enjoy causing your brother stress."

27

THE TRANSFER OF the final eight and a half million the next day was uneventful. The same six guards showed up in the same armored truck at Alvaro's hacienda to move the money while Alvaro took me aside to make the same admonishments—veiled threats, in plainer language—that I should take good care of his money or he would be very unhappy, and I replied with the same reassurances that he'd heard a few hundred times before and still did not believe.

The same eight bank employees worked with Juan Carlos to count and wire the money into the same few hundred dormant accounts in Florida; I stayed the entire day, as I always had, to make sure all the money had made it out of Mexico, and fielded the same periodic calls from Jack reporting on the status of the money that had already made it to the U.S.

When I drove away from Juan Carlos's office late that afternoon, the same shop-keepers were outside washing their side-walks, wiping their windows, locking their doors for the night. The air was littered with the same honks from angry drivers and the rancid odor of exhaust fumes as people left their offices to make their way home for the evening. Everyone was used to the routine; there were no surprises.

But life *had* changed. Dramatically. I was now not merely a prosperous man—I was very, very rich. I experienced a sense of excitement at the thought of what I had attained, but no real satisfaction, no sus-tained sense of consummation. My first thoughts were, in this order: *Man, that was fun*, and *What's next*? More. I couldn't shake the craving for it and it wasn't—to my utter astonishment—money that I was hunger-ing for. It was another look of approval from Xavier. Candace calling me her "genius boy" once again. More approbation from David. I decided that the wise thing to do would be to ground myself in something that did give me a sensation of contentment, so instead of going home when I left the bank, I drove to the school I was building.

The houses that I was having remodeled to accommodate my school were situated only about three blocks from my house. I had purchased three homes that were joined by common walls and was in the process of combining them into one large complex that would total about fourteen thousand square feet of classrooms and computer centers, a library and a language lab, dorm rooms and a cafeteria when all was said and done. I parked in front of the construction site, locked my car, and stepped around several bags of Portland cement mix in order to access the front door and open the lock to go inside.

Most of the new plumbing and electrical had already been installed, and the new plastering on walls and ceilings was coming along apace. The original, brilliantly colorful floor tiles had all been pulled up and cleaned off and the tiles were stacked in neat piles in various corners of each room, ready to be reinstalled over new—and once again even— subflooring, which had also been raised by six inches from its original level to spare recurring damage from the flooding that came with the annual heavy rains and had caused all the damage to begin with. The large compressor for the central air conditioning I was having installed—quite an unusual feature in old buildings such as these and almost unheard of in a school for poor kids—had arrived, but I couldn't see that much progress had been made with the duct work. I made a mental note to put that on my list of things I wanted to talk to the contractor about.

The school was designed for boys only—mostly because of the way I'd had to arrange the dormitory area. Perhaps a girls' wing could be added as part of the expansion my new wealth would allow? In the first year the school would serve only those kids who were between six and twelve years old; adding grades using levels of American high schools as my model was another area in which I planned for the school to grow. For now, seventy-five little boys of elementary school age would live at the school in small but clean and comfortable rooms, two to a room, in which they would each have their own narrow bed, and their own desk. I knew that the Mayan kids I wanted to serve were plenty smart, certainly as smart as any other group of kids in Mexico, but they'd never had the money or the time or the basic sort of security that would allow them to take advantage of their gifts. The Spanish weren't going to help them up the food chain; they thought of the Mayans as little more than slaves.

The kids at my school, however, equipped with a good, basic education as well as fluency in English, would be able to land good jobs with the American companies doing business in South America—companies who were always looking for talented people who could bridge the language divide. The kids who graduated from my school would have at least some of the same advantages that rich Spanish boys, like Alvaro, were born into.

At each end of each dormitory hallway was one slightly larger room, reserved for the school's teachers. I wanted my teachers—most of whom I was importing from America, at least for the first few years—to live with the kids. To be on-call for them when they needed help at night with their studies, or had a personal challenge about which they needed advice. To expose the kids to extracurricular activities and take them on field trips—reading a book before bed or going to the symphony in the evening—to show them what life could be like when a person wasn't living in poverty, was fighting to live a fulfilling life instead of only for one's next meal.

I was standing in one of the small student rooms, realizing that one of the things I was actually looking forward to doing was sitting down with the decorator my architect had recommended and choosing the furnishings for these rooms—colorful desk lamps and comfortable desk chairs and bright plaid comforters—when the text from Xavier came on my cell phone.

I enjoyed seeing you very much, his text read. And then a second text followed: *I hope I can see a whole lot more of you very soon.*

I knew what he was asking. Truth be told, if I hadn't been standing in my school, surrounded by the feeling of real joy this project gave me, I might have considered moving back to Florida, getting away from whatever craziness lay in store with Alvaro, and taking Xavier up on whatever it was he was offering. *It was great to see you too – maybe lunch when I'm in Miami next,* I typed back and hit send.

I had to wait only seconds before my phone dinged with his reply. *Love to have lunch, my dear Clint. Any time. Just let me know when.*

28

I PICKED DAVID AND Candace up at the Mérida airport late that Friday afternoon. Alvaro had offered his plane for their trip and Candace had warned me that she was taking full advantage of the fact that she didn't have to worry about commercial baggage handlers or making her way through customs so she was not packing light. I brought Pedro with me to handle her luggage.

I was more excited than I thought I'd be to have David and Candace arrive for a visit. They'd never seen my home before and I was looking forward to showing them where I lived—and how I lived. I would never have said, as a younger man, that I would have wanted to live in the sort of house in which I now resided—an old, lovingly restored colonial mansion with eighteen-foot ceilings. Mérida, however, had knocked me out the first time I'd laid eyes on it, and part of the reason I'd fallen for the city was— Well, Taavi. Walking along the city's clean, sun-filled streets with Taavi, marveling at its architecture, imagining the two of us living together in one of those splendid old structures. Imagining the two of us making a family together, and hosting my Florida family in our fine, loving home. Imagining how proud David and Candace would be of the life I had made for myself. I couldn't wait to buy one of the neglected old colonials in the middle of the city and give it the sort of attention and affection—not to mention the Brazilian granite and restored mahogany woodwork and the revitalized interior courtyard with a water feature and miniature palms—that it had lacked for far too long.

Pedro wrestled Candace's four suitcases into the house and down the hall to the guest suite I'd prepared for her and David, and I took my guests on a tour of my home.

"I could live like this," David said, taking in the richness of his surroundings.

I laughed, suddenly modest. "You'd change your mind quickly if we were in a hot spell. It gets to be over a hundred degrees in the season, with high humidity. Five minutes after you shower you're ready for another one."

"Huh," David allowed. "No, I wouldn't like that. South Florida's bad enough."

"But you don't mind, Clint?" Candace

asked. "You're happy living here?"

I nodded my head. "I think I'm a very lucky man, Candace."

"Ha!" David erupted, "A lucky man is never lazy! And you, Clint, are not a lazy man!"

I had just poured three glasses of a Mexican sauvignon blanc I'd bought because I thought Candace would like it, when my cell phone rang.

Alvaro.

I considered sending the call to voice mail, but he'd been so generous in sending his plane for David and Candace, I would have felt like a real jerk repaying his generosity with such indifference.

"Hey," I said when I answered.

"The bull," he answered. "I fought a new one today and it is just as crazy as the other ones!"

His bullfight was scheduled to take place on Sunday and he'd been in the ring with a variety of bulls every day for the last week, sharpening his skills for the big day.

"I think, Clint"—he lowered his voice—"I worry that someone is making sure I get only the crazy bulls."

I excused myself with a nod to David and Candace and went out to the patio before I answered him. "Why do you think someone would do that, Alvaro?"

"To kill me! To see that I get killed by a crazy bull!"

I swallowed, hard. The bull wasn't the only one who was crazy. If I'd thought there was any chance in hell that Alvaro was actually seeing a professional to try to correct his erratic behavior I would have thought he was off his meds again.

"I need to see you, Clint, I need you to come here to my house right now."

"Alvaro, don't you remember? David and Candace, they've just arrived—"

"Don't give me shit! Do you want to see me killed? Right now!"

I left David and Candace in Pedro's hands. "I won't be long," I told them, bringing in the rest of the sauvignon blanc in a terra cotta chiller, and topping off their glasses. "Pedro is getting some cheese and crackers ready for you—are you sure you don't mind if I step out for an hour. Maybe two?"

I arrived at the hacienda to find Alvaro's wife, Sofia, in the middle of renovating the old money bedroom, shouting at a couple of workers about using the wrong paint color on the walls, his two boys in the patio fighting and crying about whose turn it was to kick a soccer ball around the courtyard, and his henchmen huddled in the living room avoiding all three of them. "Where's Alvaro?"

One of the thugs, the one whose main position seemed to be riding shotgun whenever Alvaro was in the Hummer, jerked his thumb toward the kitchen.

"Clint! Thank you, my friend, for coming. You will see, there is something very important we must discuss!"

"So you said, Alvaro, but you know I've got David and Candace at my house and it's just plain rude to up and leave them—"

"Someone is trying to kill me and you are worried about being rude?"

I sighed and took a seat in the chair opposite him at the kitchen table. "Why do you think someone is trying to kill you?"

"Too many close calls with crazy bulls in the practice ring this week."

I nodded, and kept my voice low, to keep him calm. "But, surely, Alvaro, you're a bullfighter—you've had close calls before?"

"In all my years, only two," he answered, and rolled his eyes as if he was looking heavenward for someone to thank for saving him on these other two occasions. He pulled his shirt out of his jeans to show me the scar on his lower stomach where a bull had trampled him. "A cowboy had to get between the two of us or the bull would have stomped me to death!" He let his shirt fall over his stomach again and put his hands together, in imitation of prayer. "I have this same cowboy working for me in the fight on Sunday."

"Well, that should make you feel better—"

Alvaro ignored me and stood up and dropped his pants. "There is this one, too."

The second scar was on his upper thigh, too close to his manhood, and merely the idea of having a wild animal that close to such an area of the body made me flinch.

"The bull," Alvaro explained, "lowered his big head and came at me, gored me, threw me off to the side like I was a rag doll. The pain was so great I almost cried—which would have made my humiliation complete—"

"But you didn't, Alvaro. You didn't lose your manhood, or your dignity, or your nerve, either. How many people would have the balls to go back into a ring with a killer bull after an accident like that? Not too many, right? But you do."

The ego stroke seemed to calm him. He rubbed the scar on his thigh and said, without looking up at me, "I'm worried that if something happens to me on Sunday no one will know about my money I just transferred."

"Well, Alvaro, the money's in a bank account with your name on it. Why not just give your wife the bank account information and Jack will take care of getting the money to her if you're... you know, incapacitated. Or worse." I gave him a small smile, hoping a little gallows humor would dissipate his anxiety.

"What worse?" he bellowed.

Wrong strategy.

Before I could backtrack Alvaro stepped out of his jeans and slumped on a kitchen chair, becoming suddenly as sullen as he was manic just moments before. "It could happen. The worst? That could happen because these fucking bulls are crazy in the head. Yesterday, the bull broke down the barriers in his stall and then ran all through the spectator area of the arena. It took every cowboy in the place to round him up."

I wanted to put my head in my hands and shake the hell out of it. If he was so worried about *the worst* coming to pass, what the hell was he doing fighting any kind of a bull? And why, after knowing me for less than two weeks, was I suddenly the one who got the call when he needed to be stroked and cajoled before a fight? Where was Javier? Wasn't he the more logical choice? When had I become Alvaro's best friend?

"Look," I said, valiantly resisting the urge to shake my head, "call your lawyer first thing in the morning. Get him to make a codicil to your will—including instructions for me on what to do if your wife needs to access that money. That will take care of all your problems."

Alvaro nodded. "Well, not *all* my problems," he said, but he smiled for the first time since I'd come over that night.

I allowed myself a smile in return, which caused him to laugh. It was such a mad laugh, such a loose, blustering series of cackles and guffaws I had to join him.

"You are crazy, Clint, my friend!" he said as we laughed together. "Why would I have a will? I am going to live forever!"

29

O N SATURDAY MORNING we drove down to Xum-
al, so I could show David and Candace
the Mayan ruins there. We took our lunch in
town, at one of my most favored restaurants,
David and me nursing an extra after-lunch
shot of fine, sipping tequila while Candace
made the rounds of the shops, accumulating
more and more goods—a Yucatecan cook-
book, a hammock from Tixkokob, several
guayaberas for David, a small tinwork *Dia
de Muertos* tableaux—to cram into her luggage for the trip home. By afternoon it was
too hot to do much more than sit around
my courtyard alternating between lying on
loungers and sipping cool cocktails and taking dips in the pool—which was a way of life
down here in the hottest months of the year.

Our plan had been to enjoy the light sup-
per that Pedro had prepared for us and then

go to bed early, so we were fresh and rested for the central event the next day, the bullfight that was scheduled to begin at noon. Not one of us got much sleep at all.

In Mérida there was a celebration of some sort at least once a week. The cause of the festivities could be the election of a new president or someone buying his first car, a young girl turning fifteen or Christ rising from the cross. The national enthusiasm to celebrate was one of the reasons I fell for Mexico in the first place—I loved the warmth and authenticity and generosity of the people, their consuming desire to share life milestones with food and music and dance. But the celebrations were often impromptu, and that evening's was downright inconvenient. From about seven PM we were aware of merriment in the square—happy voices as well as the aromas of home cooking drifting through the few streets to my door. At nine we heard fireworks going off on the other side of the cathedral in the town's square—not an uncommon location for fireworks, I'd discovered, though the cathedral was rarely without at least two or three penitents inside and I often wondered how the fireworks helped their prayers. After the fireworks ended, the Mariachi music started, broadcast from enormous boom boxes set up around the square, the dancing and drinking notched up a level, and the party began in earnest.

Candace thought it was charming, teasing her "two cranky men" that we should join in the spirit of celebration too, insisting we make margaritas and raise our glasses to whatever it was the people on the street were so happy about—until two in the morning. At that hour, even Candace gave in to her own weariness. We all took a chilly swim, then sat around the cabana and drank the dregs of our cocktails until, at last, at four in the morning, the noise subsided. If Pedro hadn't been there to wake us in the morning we might have slept through Alvaro's fight.

The three of us dressed lightly, in shorts and short-sleeved shirts, Candace's of crisp, white linen that I knew would crumple as the heat and the day wore on. We wore hats on our heads in defense against the blazing sun, and Candace slathered our noses and David's bald spot with sunscreen for good measure.

We left my house by 10:30 to head to the arena. Bullfights drew thousands of spectators and, I knew from experience, most of the locals, who would make up a majority of the crowd, would head to the arena about fifteen minutes before the event was scheduled to begin. They seemed to be genetically infused with a more blessed sense of time than ours that did not include the concept of "being late", or of stressing out because one was stuck in a traffic jam. But we were gringos and I made sure we were on our way long before the roads were due to become congested.

Alvaro had provided us with tickets to the event—a special valet voucher that allowed us to drive right up to the arena gate and be relieved of our car, rather than park in one of the far and dusty lots along the arena route and take a mile-long hike to the arena itself; and VIP passes that gave us entrée to his family's enclosed box that featured plush, upholstered seating rather than bleachers, air conditioning, and a small bar tended by a young Mayan boy, and from whom we could choose refreshments from a menu more extensive than I would have imagined.

David and Candace and I chose beers, and an enormous bowl of chips that we shared with Alvaro's relatives as they began to arrive. I introduced David and Candace to Alvaro's wife, and she introduced us all to the aunts and uncles, cousins and nephews and nieces and the rest who'd come to see Alvaro uphold both family tradition and honor. They greeted us in English, but soon reverted to speaking to each other in Spanish, a language that, among us, only Candace spoke fluently. She seemed to be enjoying an animated conversation with one of Alvaro's aunts, but David and I were relegated to commenting only to each other. I looked around for Javier but he was absent which, even at the time, I thought was strange. I had also held out a not-unreasonable hope of meeting Alvaro's brother, Oscar, the much more famous bullfighter in the family—we were, after all, at a bullfighting arena, Oscar's stomping grounds, so to speak, and Alvaro had given me a shrug and a "Maybe" when I'd mentioned the possibility to him on Friday night, but he wasn't among the throng of relatives gathered that day either.

In the ring a teen-aged boy and a small bull were putting on an exhibition fight. The boy had no sword, only a cape, and the young bull was bouncing around the ring as if he believed the two of them were playing and having great fun.

"Poor thing," I said to David because, for all my desire to see the first bullfight of my life, I was well aware of the protests around the sport; and I hadn't reconciled myself at all to what was the essential brutality of it. "He has no idea the bull's fate is to take a sword through his skull."

David, older and more resigned, sighed. "Well, you know, when the bull is killed it's taken to a slaughter house and made into steaks. The meat won't go to waste."

By the time the exhibition was over, twenty thousand people had poured into the arena to see the main attraction: Alvaro's battle with a grown and widely-reputed-to-be-ferocious bull. Television cameras from the three major local networks had set up to broadcast the event to all the sorry souls who had the ill-luck not to be here in person. Trumpets, drum beats, and twenty thousand voices raised in approval as a parade of local horsemen began—fifty prime specimens of horse flesh decked out in colored blankets and headgear made of silver and strung with feathers, strutting single file around the perimeter of the arena, their owners sitting tall and proud in their saddles, an over-sized Mexican flag fluttering over the head of the man astride the lead horse. It was a moving spectacle; I would never have expected that I would feel so much excitement at a bullfight, especially before the bull came out.

The horse parade was followed by the entrance of the four cowboys who would protect Alvaro, riding their horses at full speed around and around the perimeter of the ring, kicking up clouds of dust. With the arrival of the cowboys, the crowd, nearly to a person, jumped out of their seats and began to stomp their feet and cry, "Alvaro! Al-va-ro!"

When Alvaro emerged from the dugout

directly beneath our VIP seats, he did so with a customary flourish. His thick, black hair curled around his temples, his neck and his forehead where his *sombrero de matador* sat lightly on his head; and his tights looked as if he had been poured into them—his cock bulging, his ass high and round as he paraded to the center of the ring, waving regally and making a full circle to bow to each section of the adoring audience chanting his name. I had no idea he had such a devoted following; even Candace gasped at his beauty.

I was so mesmerized by the sight of him that it took the sudden hush of the crowd to draw me back to the action—the biggest bull I had ever seen came charging from a gate across the arena from where Alvaro stood looking suddenly very small and vulnerable. The bull raged as if someone had just tried to brand him with a hot iron. Alvaro stood, stoic and proud, in the center of the ring and swirled his cape around him so it flowed like a skirt. The bull charged at full speed, narrowing the gap between bull and matador, tearing through the cape as the crowd let out a gasp, raising dust under his feet and around Alvaro, the red cape fluttering through the haze as the bull sped by his adversary. As the dust settled, Alvaro twirled the cape to his waist and raised an arm in the air and threw back his head, erect and strong and, to my mystified eyes, unscathed. The crowd erupted, and clamored for more.

Alvaro indulged them as the bull, confused and even angrier because of it, turned back to him. Alvaro held the red cape in both hands, waist-level, and let it sway slowly, teasing the beast, hunting the bull as much as the bull hunted him, daring the bull to come at him. I saw his mouth move, as if he was taunting, "Bring it, you fat bastard."

The next charge by the bull came even closer to Alvaro, and the next even closer than that, allowing Alvaro to demonstrate his dangerous trick of seeming to be turned by the bull as it sped past him, emerging from charge after charge with his arms lifted in triumph, and a smile on his face.

When Alvaro drew his sword, the crowd roared in anticipation, and the bull charged. I saw Candace close her eyes, unwilling to witness the bull's final confrontation, Alavaro's sword plunging into its neck. But Alvaro swirled the cape before him as the bull neared, twirling it away once more as the bull sped by, flashing the cape and taunting the bull into ever tightening circles around him, passing by the opportunity spin after spin to plunge the sword into the animal's flesh.

We, in the crowd, were breathing as one, with Alvaro, drawing in air in gulps and holding it, tense, until the bull completed another circle around Alvaro when we sighed it out, the sound like the soundtrack of ocean swells behind the ballet of the matador.

The exhausted bull loped around the ring, dazed by Alvaro's magic, limply pawing the dust with a forefoot, not yet ready to give up. Alvaro looked to our booth, to the two young boys sitting in the front row of it, his sons. He held his gaze, asking the silent question of them: *Does the bull die?*

My eyes shifted to the boys. I was surprised by the depth of the relief I felt as I saw them shaking their heads vigorously: *No! No, Papi!*

Alvaro nodded his assent and, with one almost imperceptible tilt of his head to his cowboys, the chute was opened and the miserable animal was herded back into its pen. I expected, for one twitchy second, that the spectators would be disappointed Alvaro had spared the beast, but a bright, loud cheer of appreciation for the matador's gallantry rose from the stands, the audience standing as one, the men waving their hats and the women throwing red roses in the air that landed like drops of blood in the dust by Alvaro's feet.

Alvaro pulled off his own hat to toss it in the air. His curls were wet, matted to his brow and neck and he shook his head to loosen them, then ran a hand through his hair to pull it off his face. The four cowboys returned to the center of the ring, leading a titanic, unsaddled black stallion among them. In one swift movement Alvaro had mounted the Spanish Paso. He kicked the horse and set off on a victory gallop around the arena. A towel came flying out of the stands as Alvaro passed by. He plucked it out of the air, wiped his face with it, and tossed it back into the throng where it would become someone's prized souvenir. I felt lightheaded, the excitement and the heat and the heady odor of horse sweat wafting from the ring; I wondered that Alvaro didn't simply pass out at the sheer volume of admiration and lust being directed at him.

"What did you think of it, honey?" I heard David ask Candace as they applauded along with all the thousands of us.

"I hated every minute of it," Candace whispered, adding reverently, "and I think I just had an orgasm."

Exactly, I thought.

It takes a while for twenty thousand people to exit an arena, especially when the matador they've come to see is standing in full view, glistening with sweat and victory, one arm around his beautiful wife, his youngest son hoisted up in the crook of the other.

They knew they had to leave, the event was over, but they moved slowly, turning their heads and craning their necks and letting their eyes linger on the day's hero.

David and Candace and I stood in the background of the VIP booth, not wanting to get in the way of Alvaro's family and fans. We occupied a space that day somewhere above the hoi polloi but below his doting aunts and proud uncles. Besides, he had invited us to a party that evening to celebrate his victory over the bull, so we had no need to crowd around him now; we'd get plenty of face time with the idol this evening.

As we waited for the crowd to thin so we could make our way outside and claim my car from the valet, my cell began to vibrate in my pocket.

"Hey, Jack."

"What's all that noise?"

"The bullfight! I can't explain it, you have to see one for yourself to understand what it feels like around here right now, but Alvaro won—and no injuries. Your mother—"

"Clint, tell me about it later. Can you go somewhere where you can hear me? We need to talk—Abe is in the middle of a royal fucking shit fit."

30

ALVARO, DISAPPOINTED WE were not going to stay for his victory party but too flush with the victory itself to ask too many questions, readily offered his plane so David, Candace, and I could make an emergency trip north.

"Great, Alvaro, thank you—can you call your pilot right now and tell him we're on our way?" I asked, over my shoulder, already moving through the crowd at the arena, Moses parting the Red Sea, David and Candace following closely in my wake. I handed the attendant at the gate my valet parking voucher and a fifty dollar bill—"There's one more just like that if you get my Land Rover here in less than five minutes." The attendant was only too happy to oblige.

I called Pedro on my cell phone as I drove, instructing him to have the Cohens' luggage ready and waiting at the curb, and to throw together a duffle with my toiletries and a couple of changes of clothes for me—I would be pulling up in about twenty minutes to collect everything.

"I believe we are in the midst of a bit of an overreaction," Candace said as I manhandled the luggage away from Pedro and into the back of the Land Rover and then drove twenty miles over the speed limit toward the Mérida airport.

"I agree." This from David, alone in the backseat, worrying an unlit cigarette—the first one he'd taken out of the pack he carried in his breast pocket since he'd come to Mexico—between his fingers. "I told you, I've already taken care of this. What Abe does doesn't matter."

I wove in between cars, changing lanes, dodged a small taxi that tried to cut me off, returned a middle finger to the driver I'd pissed off.

"Really, Clint."

"I'm sorry, Candace."

"I mean, why are you so frightened of Abe all of a sudden."

"He talked to the Feds!"

The tires squealed as I took the turn onto the road marked *Private Jets Only* a little too tightly and headed for Alvaro's hangar.

"As I said," David repeated, bracing himself against the door to counter the force of my errant turn, "I've talked to the people who are auditing the bank—as long as we can pull the bank out of the fire, keep it from going under and needing a bail out, they don't care where the money comes from. There is no reason to fear whatever it is that Abe's done."

"I don't *fear* Abe," I said, throwing my car into park at the door to the hangar. "I am angry with Abe. And he ought to fear me."

"Coffee," I barked at Tim as we boarded. I felt immediately like a heel, venting my fury on Tim, but not enough to take the time to explain or apologize. "Two black, one with cream." I told him—and added, "Please."

"Yes, sir." Tim scurried to comply.

"I can't believe Xavier would tell Abe we sold the bank shares to you." David batted the low, gold table with his hand.

Candace put her hand on her husband's arm. "I can't believe he and Abe ran into each other at Pascal's! Xavier going so downscale..."

"And Abe eating a meal that didn't include a Big Mac?" I asked.

"I ought to call that son of a bitch right now and fire his ass." David's hands were clenched into fists. "That deal was not his to divulge. I should report him to the bar."

I shook my head. "Miami's a small town—

like every other town on the face of the earth, you travel in a certain circle and you're eventually going to run into all the other people who travel in it too. We never told him the deal was a secret in any way. He and Abe run into each other, Abe brings up the idea of him investing in the bank again, Xavier laughs and wonders why there's a need for an investor now that I'm part owner... And if you fire Xavier you give up the best attorney in the state. You're getting mad at the wrong person, David."

David balled his hands together, Candace still gripping his arm for support.

"What we've done so far with Alvaro," I said, "is only the beginning. He's still in business, making more money every day. And he isn't the only businessman in Mexico who's making a lot of money every day—and all of that money will need a new home. We're not talking twenty million, David. We're talking forty, eighty, a hundred million. Or more. Think of what we could do with all of that money—beyond just enriching all of us. My business partners—" I hesitated, thinking how to phrase what I wanted to say without blatantly spilling what that business actually was to Candace. "My business partners aren't going to just *stop*; with or without our involvement they aren't going to just stop making money... But because of us, that money is going to be in the states. And so much of it is going to have to be spent in the states! That money could renovate whole neighborhoods in Florida, bring whole towns back to life, give whole cities of American workers employment! Renovate churches, and pave roads, and build schools—my share of just this first deal is going to make it possible for me to expand my school in Mérida beyond my wildest dreams! Think of the possibilities!"

David and Candace were as breathless as I was at this point.

"Abe may be a gnat circling our ass right now, but he could turn into a real pest as our deposits start to grow. The Feds won't look the other way forever, not when so much money is involved, and not if Abe keeps making a nuisance of himself. Eventually someone will pay attention to him. We've got to shut him down. Tonight."

31

"**T**ELL US WHAT you know, Jack."

We were seated around the island in the Cohens' kitchen. Candace had brewed a fresh pot of coffee, and Jack had gone to the liquor cabinet and pulled out a bottle of whiskey to spike the caffeine.

"I don't know much," Jack began. "Sharon called me last week—out of the blue, you know? She asked me to have lunch with her. I mean, when was the last time we were willingly together under the same roof when we didn't have to be?"

Sharon had asked Jack to meet her in Coral Gables, at a Cuban sandwich shop where they had the least chance of running into one of Abe's banking associates, or any of the ladies from her various social or charitable organizations. They'd ordered two Cubanos and taken a table in the back.

Sharon's family background was financially modest, but religiously, they were extravagantly abundant. Sharon had grown up attending church three times a week—twice on Sundays—arriving in her family's battered, pre-owned SUV, dressed in ill-fitting clothes from second-hand stores, crammed in the back among seven brothers, all of whom, because they were boys, got more of their parents' attention and larger portions at the dinner table.

When Sharon met Abe in high school—fat and unathletic, unpopular and not particularly bright, but richer than anyone Sharon had ever known—she knew that she could have him if she wanted him, and if she had him she would never have to shop at thrift stores again. She didn't love him, but she could live with him—and all he could provide.

Sharon was Abe's first sexual conquest—if you called ejaculating on yourself a conquest; Abe's problem had delayed her plans. It had taken her months longer to get pregnant than she had thought it would, but once she was certain that she was she told her parents immediately, and they had gone quickly and indignantly to Abe's parents to demand he do the right thing. David and Candace had been unequivocal: Abe and Sharon were going to have this baby, and they would do everything within their power to help the new, young couple. That had included buying them a small house and providing a monthly allowance while they both finished high school, and Abe got his degree in business management at the University of Miami. Ten months before his college graduation Abe had his first affair, with a fellow student in his business law class. Sharon couldn't put her finger on it but she sensed that Abe was becoming distracted from the life she wanted to build for herself, so nine months before his college graduation, Sharon "accidentally" got pregnant again. Three weeks after the graduation ceremony, thanks to a nanny arranged for by Candace, she and Abe took their first real vacation together—five days on the island of Maui, compliments of the Cohens—and the day after they got back, Abe started working at the bank for his father.

At least that was how Jack and I had always understood their story; we'd had plenty of good laughs over the years at the ease with which the unschooled, unsophisticated Sharon had manipulated his big brother, and how anyone with two more neurons than Abe possessed would have seen through her in a nanosecond. On the other hand, we also knew damned well what the attraction was for Abe. Sharon had been willing to live without love, without joy or passion, in exchange for a lifetime of financial security, but she had always lived without respect: she had been raised to be submissive to her father, her brothers, and her husband. Abe appreciated the deference she offered to him as head of the family, and he absolutely savored the superiority his new religion bestowed upon him over anyone who deviated from norms they had decided upon: white, heterosexual, conservative Christians. The sense of power was addictive.

Sharon was paying a heavy price for her material comfort—I knew; Xavier had tried to extract the same price from me once upon a time. But from what she had told Jack over their Cubanos the week before, she was starting to feel as if her tab had been paid in full.

"She thinks Abe's screwing around on her again," Jack told us. "She wanted my help in finding out for sure." He laughed, lifted his cup of steaming hot coffee and took a deep breath of the whiskey before he took a sip. "I asked her what sort of help she wanted, and why in hell she thought I would want to do it. I mean, I hope she takes him for all he's got and ever hopes to get, but I'm totally uninvested in the personal life of either of them, right?

"So Sharon, this simple little fundamentalist who likes to go around pretending she doesn't have a shred of guile in her body, puts down her sandwich and leans over the table and says to me, all secret-agent, god-father, I'm-gonna-make-you-an-offer-you-can't-refuse, 'I have information about your brother that you will want to have, and I will give it to you if you help me'."

"My!" Candace whispered, but she was the only one who spoke for a good five minutes.

"What do you think she could mean?" David broke the silence.

Jack shrugged. "No idea. Gave her an STD? Has a slew of unpaid parking tickets? Killed someone?"

"Stop it, Jack," his mother commanded.

"Anyway, I hired a retired cop and he's been tailing Abe for three days now to see if we can find out how he's spending his spare time—"

"Have you found out anything?" I asked before his parents could rebuke him.

"Nothing yet. Except, Clint, you'll never guess who Sharon's made an appointment with to, you know, get her ducks in a row if she does decide she needs a divorce."

"You've got to be kidding me..."

"Our family's giving Xavier a lot of business lately."

32

"I THINK ALVARO HAS a thing for you." Candace had put away the coffee pot and we were now drinking our whiskey with sweet vermouth and bitters. Candace was teasing a maraschino cherry out of her glass with a long, elegant manicured finger. The information Jack had shared with us about Abe—and his proactive response to it—had calmed me considerably; spending the night as the Cohens' guest, visiting with these people I loved over perfect Manhattans while we awaited delivery of a large pepperoni-with-extra-cheese pizza from the joint that had been my favorite since I was a kid—this seemed like a well-deserved reward. I could relax this evening; Abe was on everyone's radar. "I saw the way Alvaro looked at you..."

"Oh, I didn't notice a thing." David emphasized his point with a dismissive wave of his hand. Of course, unless it had been a drop-dead gorgeous woman making a direct pass at him, David *wouldn't* have noticed. "Besides, Candace, he's married. Two kids." He laughed. "Get real."

It never failed to amaze me, the way people could be so unimaginative—as if someone's being married locked up their sexuality in a neat little box. The way they accepted people's facades just the way they were intended to be received, at face value.

"Well," Jack added, "he certainly seemed straight to me, too. I asked him to go out and hit South Beach with me when he was here, but he said he'd take a rain check. The next time he was in Miami, he said, after all the money was transferred, we'd go out on a pussy hunt—"

"Jack!"

"Sorry, Mom. Alvaro's word, not mine. Anyway, I didn't pick up anything about Alvaro on my gaydar."

"Really?" I asked.

"Oh, but you know how the Spanish are, in any case," David added, waving a hand again and knocking it into his crystal glass, which Candace deftly reached out to right before it toppled over. "All touchy-feeling, hugging and kissing each other. It's a Mediterranean thing, you know?"

"I know you're a little tipsy, that's what

I know," his wife told him, and moved his glass back a few inches on the counter, out of the way of his expressive hands.

We were all a little tipsy by that point in the evening, which was why not one of us heard a car pull into the driveway or the door to the kitchen open, or noticed Abe standing by it until he spoke.

"Hell of a thing to come home to, half my inheritance sold to a fucking faggot."

"Oh, dear," Candace murmured.

"And not just that—oh, no! I've been to the bank, I've looked over the activity on your brand-new account, you little queer." Abe sputtered as he spoke, resting a hand on the doorframe and leaning into it in an attempt to keep his balance; apparently he was even tipsier than any of us. "Tell me, how's a cocksucker like you come into four million dollars in less than a week?"

"Language, Abe," his mother warned.

"You know"—Jack held up an admonishing finger—"we really prefer to be called trouser pilots these days."

"Yeah, well, your little pilot buddy over here is going to jail—it can't be legal, whatever he did to get four million dollars, and I have the Feds looking into it."

"Ach!" The guttural sound coming from David was thick with disgust. "You don't have the Feds doing anything, Abe, except laughing behind your back about what a jackass you are—"

"You wouldn't have an inheritance any more at all if Clint hadn't stepped up." This from Candace.

"But why *him!*" Abe cried. It was a noise I'd heard before—when I'd beaten him by over thirty seconds in the quarter mile during the elementary school intramural track meet when I was in fourth grade and he was in sixth. When I made the varsity football team as a freshman and he couldn't make first string even as a junior. When, even though I was several years younger than he was, I passed my driver's test before he did. "Why *him!* I told you I have some wealthy friends and I've been working on them to invest in the bank—your own lawyer, for example, Xavier! Why would you let a fucking fruit buy into the family business!"

Jack's head swiveled as fast as mine did, and we locked eyes, but we both managed to stifle our nearly uncontainable guffaws. I like to think I'm a discreet man, and Xavier's secret certainly wasn't mine to divulge, but I was fairly sure that it was only the doorbell ringing, announcing the delivery of our pizza pie, that kept me from blurting out: "Xavier? You mean Xavier Sousa? Funny, you didn't know he was a trouser pilot too?"

33

"DAVID TOLD ME that you are greedy and that any business I have in the future can be between him and me—you won't have anything at all to do with it."

"David never said anything remotely like that."

Alvaro and I were faced off in the courtyard of his hacienda. I had driven there by myself, shortly after his summons early on the morning after I'd flown back from Miami. His wife and his kids were nowhere to be seen, and we were surrounded by his thugs, yet my certainty in David's loyalty made me feel more invulnerable than I certainly was.

"I got online like Jack told me and I was looking at my new account with sixteen million dollars in it and I think there should be twenty there. I paid you too much for a little bit of work to move my money around—you took advantage of me."

"Alvaro, I don't believe anyone's ever taken advantage of you in your life—"

"Fifty thousand, maybe, that's what it is worth to have my money moved, not four million—"

"Fifty thousand? The hoops I've had to jump through, you think I'd do that for a bullshit fifty thousand? You've got to be fucking kidding me—"

"No, I am not kidding, and you will give me my money back—all of it but your fee, fifty thousand!"

I didn't need this. Not this morning. My head had been throbbing since Jack had awakened me at the crack of dawn with the news that Abe had decided to come and visit me in Mérida.

"What can I tell you?" Jack had asked. "He was at Mom and Dad's all day yesterday. I mean, you know he passed out on the kitchen floor after he had his little hissy fit, but you left to go back to Mexico before he woke up with what was apparently the mother of all hangovers. He didn't want to face Sharon looking like something the dog had dragged around the yard, have her call him out on the sins of demon rum or something, so he just stayed at Mom and Dad's and whined to Mom all day for ice water and hot tea and aspirin and cold compresses."

I'd closed my eyes. "The point, Jack. What's the *point*? How did the idea of his coming to Mexico come up?"

"All his idea, I swear to you. He just told me he was going to fly down there, and he'd shut the fuck up and wouldn't say another word to the Feds or anyone else if you could prove to him your business is legit."

"Ah, well," I'd replied as matter-of-factly as I could manage, "you know I can't do that."

"Ah, well, you're going to have to. Planes fly to Mexico; he's a big boy and he can book a ticket. Short of handcuffing him to a drainpipe in my basement, I don't know how to stop him."

"You're just more help than the fucking Red Cross, Jack." I'd nearly broken my cell phone hanging up on him.

Now this: Alvaro pacing menacingly around his courtyard, four guys with automatic weapons on their backs eyeing him in case he wanted them to do anything—like use me for a punching bag.

Or shoot me.

"Here's the deal, Alvaro..."—my voice was surprisingly steady as I spoke—"the Cohens are good friends of mine, and I have a deal with them, too. Anything happens to me, every penny in your account gets transferred into mine. And you, a foreign drug kingpin, can take up getting it back with the U.S. Justice Department."

Not a word of it was true but, in a pinch, I can spread the bullshit as thick as I have to. I thought surely Alvaro had broken his hand, hard as he punched the adobe pillar to his left as soon as I was done speaking.

I was still shaking by the time I got home, so I popped a Sol to help me regain my equilibrium, lost my T-shirt and sandals, and flopped on a lounge chair on my patio. I had recently become a very wealthy man and I'd supposed my life was going to take on a new ease and luster because of it, but it wasn't yet even eleven AM and I badly needed a nap.

The sun was directly overhead, high noon, when I woke up soaked in sweat, blinking in surprise at Alvaro standing over me.

"What the fuck, Alvaro—"

Alvaro bent over me and gave me the biggest smile I'd ever seen on his face. "I think you need to learn to be more respectful of me and my business, my friend," he said, and then he stood up and stepped back so I could see the half dozen *Federales* standing behind him on my patio.

"What the *fuck*—"

I was stunned stupid. My hands were

shaking so badly the *Federales* had a hard time putting the handcuffs on me, but they managed. Pedro had the wherewithal to think to throw my shirt over my shoulders as I slid my feet into my sandals and the cops crowded me out my front door. I watched Alvaro stand outside my front door, rocking on his heels and laughing, and my neighbors watched me as I was herded into the back of the police truck. "Look," I said, speaking in what was still my rudimentary Spanish, "where are you taking me?"

"We are delivering you to your new home, Señor Kennedy, courtesy of Señor Alvaro Jorge Moreno."

34

THERE WAS MUCH I didn't know about the operation of drug cartels but I suspected, much like running a bank in the U.S. required that you cozy up to the Feds who were periodically sent in to audit your books, running drugs in Mexico required you have the police on your payroll. I would just need to figure out who among the police in the rat-hole of a jail Alvaro had me tossed into were on his.

I took a seat on the cell's concrete floor, sitting cross-legged and hiding a random semi-erection with the shirt Pedro had so thoughtfully thrown over my shoulders when I was marched out of my house. The air was humid and warm and smelled of human waste, and my cell mates—I would soon learn their names: Luis, Gustavo, Manuel, Jose, Carlos, and another Pedro entirely—

did not particularly excite my attraction, so I blamed the hard-on on pure adrenaline. Luis's eyes darted between my legs and a big smile revealed several missing teeth. "I think I see what I can do for you," he said to me, which was how I learned that he spoke quite passable English.

"Look," I replied, "who do I need to bribe in order to make a phone call?"

Though he was disappointed that information was all I required of him, Luis made the bargain deal with the youngest and tidiest looking jailer of five hundred pesos in exchange for three minutes of phone time.

"You need to call your attorney?" the young man asked, leaning close to me through the bars of the cell. I could tell exactly what he'd had for lunch when he spoke, but I didn't want to offend him by covering my nose with my hand. The truth was, now that I was going to get to use the phone, I wasn't sure at all who to call. I'd have told you, just a week before, that my few weeks of political activism had made me a boatload of friends in high places in Mérida but, when push came to shove, I wasn't sure which ones of them were my friends and which ones were Alvaro's. Pedro—my houseboy, not my cellmate—was the only person I knew I could absolutely trust in all of Mexico, but if he had the power to get me sprung from this hellhole he would also have had the power to keep me from being thrown in jail in the first place.

"Hey, Señor," the young guard with mind-altering halitosis repeated, "you need to call your attorney?"

"No," I told him. "I need to call my architect."

I called Miguel, and Miguel called Pablo and, within the hour, Pablo was the one who was talking to me from outside my rotten jail cell. He had his white linen blazer draped over his shoulders so, in deference to the filth of the place, he stood back while the young and tidy guard unlocked the door so I could exit. "*Vuelve pronto*," my cellmates called to me, Luis adding, "*Vuelve pronto a verme!*"

"It was a pleasure, boys," I called back as the cell door clanked behind me.

"Alvaro Moreno got you into this?" Pablo asked as we walked briskly down the hallway of the jail and into the hot, sticky, fresh air of freedom.

"He did."

Pablo made a disparaging sound as he clicked his keychain and unlocked the doors of his fresh-from-the-factory Cadillac Escalade. He told me to get inside and then went around the back of the car to slide in behind the wheel himself. It was remarkable to me that he had come alone to the jail to see to my release, and that he was driving his own vehicle—this had not, up until that moment, been my experience of how a drug kingpin went about his daily travels. Kingpins, so far as I had seen, traveled in packs, within drawing distance of their hired guns.

"I would give my left testicle for a hot shower," I said, and made Pablo laugh.

"We never know what we may be asked to give up for the things we want," he said, "but, for today, I am taking you to your home where you may shower as well as keep both your nuts."

"For that, I am most grateful."

"Even so, I must ask you something," he said while negotiating the turn onto Mérida's main highway.

"Of course."

"Why are you working for Alvaro?"

It was a question I didn't know how to answer. It occurred to me that my ignorance of how drug cartels worked included not knowing what kind of bad blood—what kind of rivalry—might lie between my employer and his competitor who had just bailed me out of jail.

"Alvaro Moreno, Señor Kennedy, is, as your American saying goes, small potatoes, and he is also a very crazy man, and I want you to explain to me why it is worth it to you to put up with such a big crazy for such a small man."

I tried to formulate my response—because twenty million dollars is a lot of potatoes to me!—but before I could, I heard what sounded like a car backfiring on the corner behind us, and a nanosecond later the upper part of the driver's side window of Pablo's car shattered, and Pablo shouted, "Get down!" as he reached around my head, shoved it to the floor of the passenger side of the vehicle, and stomped on the gas.

I lay on the plush carpeting of Pablo's car listening to tires squealing, metal crashing, horns honking, several more gunshots and my heart beating as if it was working harder than it could take.

"That was close," Pablo conceded, waving at me to come out from under my seat and onto the street where a crowd had gathered around a lone gunman laying prone on the concrete in front of a neighborhood taqueria. "Who do you think could have tipped off Alvaro that you were released from jail?" he asked me.

"No one. No one I can think of. Certainly not Miguel..."

"Of course not Miguel," Pablo said and pulled me from the Cadillac at the corner of Avenida Reforma and Paseo de Monteio, where the Escalade had crashed after the car had taken a bullet in its windshield and Pablo had careened it into the stand of a fruit vendor who stood as shaken and dumbfounded as I was myself, but unhurt, though his cart looked as if it had been put through a crusher at a chop shop.

Two *Federales* stood over the man who was lying face-down on the concrete. They had already cuffed him and, before he'd passed out cold, he'd responded by pissing in his tan cotton slacks—a development I could both see and smell.

"I am so sorry about your new car, Señor Pablo," one of the cops said to my savior, brushing a piece of non-existent dust from Pablo's pristine white blazer. In Mexico, the average policeman earned three hundred dollars American per month. The cartel bosses had an easy time buying the loyalty of the police; providing each policeman with an additional three hundred dollars a month doubled their salaries, and counted for peanuts in the cartel's accounting.

Pablo waved him off. "Señor Kennedy, I think you know this man?"

My legs felt hollow but somehow I made them work and made my way over to Pablo and the cowering man on the sidewalk. As I approached, Pablo kicked the man under his shoulder so hard he flipped over on his back. "Oh, my God," I gasped. "Javier!"

One of the *Federales*, the one who stood closest to Pablo with his arms folded over his chest, asked, "What do you want us to do with this guy."

Pablo looked at me for an instant, as if I might have an answer, then shrugged and said, "Throw him in my car. I might have a few questions I want to ask of him when he wakes up."

35

JAVIER WOKE SLOWLY, opening his crusted eyelids, lifting his cuffed hands to rub the back of his head, looking incredulously at the blood and bits of hair on his hand.

Pablo drove cautiously, constantly adjusting his position in order to have any kind of adequate view through the splintered windshield, only glancing in the rearview mirror as we heard Javier begin to move in the backseat.

"What I want to know, Javier," he said, "is who called you. Who called Alvaro to let him know Señor Kennedy had been released from jail?" He paused, then added, "Which guard betrayed me?"

Javier averted his eyes, looking out the back passenger window into the middle distance, a man already ruined and resigned to the worst. "I've got to shit," he said.

"Do not shit in my car unless you want to eat it," Pablo told him, and turned off the highway onto a dirt road that led to his hacienda.

The road was lined with small, concrete block, tin-roofed shacks, grubby little pot-bellied kids, nursing mothers, and starving dogs in the patches of mud and weeds that passed for their front yards. Their husbands, I suspected, worked for Pablo, tending his house and his grounds, though likely none of them were married to the more prosperous-looking men who carried automatic weapons and guarded the main entrance to the hacienda. As the wounded Escalade pulled through the arched hacienda entrance, two guards rushed to open its doors—one for Pablo, and one for me.

"Get that piece of shit out of the back," Pablo instructed the guard who'd opened his door. "Put him in the room behind the pool, and don't do any more harm to him. Poor thing, he has been through enough this afternoon," he laughed. "And I want him conscious to answer the questions I have for him."

Javier didn't struggle as the guards yanked him from the backseat of the Escalade. He was a man resigned to his fate, whatever that might be, a sort of courage I likened to that of a medieval lord going to his death praising his king so that his family wouldn't be slaughtered as well. It momentarily increased my esteem for Javier, until Pablo said, "You know that he knows I'm not going to have him killed?"

"He does?" I felt an immediate sense of relief—I was, at heart, a pampered American businessman and all of my current associations suddenly seemed too medieval for my comfort. I also reacted to Pablo's mercy with a cruel sense of injustice: he tried to kill *us*!

"No, no," Pablo assured me, walking me to one of the guest rooms in his expansive hacienda so I could clean up. "He is much more valuable to me alive."

I stood under the shower in Pablo's guest room for a good fifteen minutes. I'd spent only little more than an hour in that grimy, Mexican jail, but it felt as if I had to wash off a month of filth. When I emerged from the shower, dressed in the fresh clothes Pablo had his minions lay out for me—a pair of khaki shorts and a white, Oxford-cloth sport shirt that fit surprisingly well, considering they were ordered up for me on short notice—Pablo met me in his courtyard.

It was only then, once again clean and clear-headed, that I took in the splendor of Pablo's hacienda. The size and scope of the space dwarfed even Alvaro's impressive

spread; the variety of the flora, and the intricate plan of their planting, exceeded geomet-
rically the thoughtfulness of the landscape
architect Alvaro had employed. Alvaro's
place looked like the most well-designed
Courtyard Marriot you had ever seen; Pablo's looked like the Southern Hemisphere's
answer to Versailles.

Pablo was waiting for me, seated at a
wrought-iron table, nursing a Cuban and a
heavy, lead-crystal glass filled with amber
liquid. "Armagnac," he said, lifting his glass.
"Will you have some?"

"Love to."

Pablo poured from a decanter set on the
middle of the table and offered the glass to
me as he spoke. "Here is what I have learned,
Clint," he said. "I have learned that you have
performed a great service for Alvaro, but that
he is proving to be ungrateful to you for it."

I took a sip of the Armagnac. It was not
my favorite beverage, but it felt bracing at
the moment—just what I needed.

"I believe that you will find the volume
of business that I can offer you far exceeds
what Alvaro was able to supply." He rolled the
cigar around in his mouth and took a puff,
exhaling a perfect smoke ring. He watched it
billow and dissipate before continuing. "I believe that you will also find I am much more
appreciative of the services rendered to me

than Alvaro could ever be. That is because, while Alvaro is very handsome, and a good bullfighter, he does not have much of a business head. I mean," Pablo clarified, "he is too crazy in the head to be good at business."

I listened intently, and found myself nodding as Pablo talked. "I have spoken with Javier at length," he said and, when I frowned—the question, When did you get to speak with him *at length?* hanging in the air—he shrugged. "At least, I talked to him while you were in the shower— Have you noticed that Javier seemed absent lately from Alvaro's inner circle?"

I nodded that, yes, I had.

"A-huh, well, many people have noticed this. Javier tells me it is because Alvaro has taken it into his head that Javier is stealing from him. Skimming money from the street dealers who sell for him—not reporting the full amounts that are taken in each day and lining his pockets with the difference. I have to tell you, Clint, I find such a scenario most impossible—Javier is a beautiful man, but timid. Much too cowardly to steal from his brother-in-law."

Pablo shook his head, and ashed his cigar in a silver ashtray set on a small table behind him before he continued. "Alvaro wanted Javier to prove his loyalty, and he found a way this afternoon that he thought was brilliant—as only crazy men can think of such things. The guard you bribed today in order to get a message to me?"

I took another sip of my Armagnac, bracing for what was to come.

"Clint, that guard called Alvaro as soon as you had made your call to Miguel, to tell him that I was on my way to set you free. Alvaro sent Javier to prove his loyalty by harming you."

The words—my whole life—seemed surreal in that moment. My hand slipped from my crystal glass of Armagnac and I sat, frozen. Even alcohol wasn't going to help thaw me out.

Pablo let me sit like that for several minutes. Then he stubbed out his cigar in the silver ashtray and reached a hand over and placed it on top of mine. "There are four major drug cartels in Eastern Mexico. Those of us who run these organizations, we have many, you might say, *sub-contractors* who work for us. Alvaro's sub-contraction business is under my flag, and it is the least in size, because he is the most unpredictable. It is difficult for an unpredictable boss to retain loyal employees for any length of time. I believe you should come and work directly for me, and for my friends, too. I believe you will find ours to be a, how do you say it? Less hostile work environment."

I couldn't immediately respond to the offer; the fact that you have been targeted for assassination doesn't enter you intellectually—it is a physical knowledge. And then when I was done throwing up at the base of a really lush, pink rhododendron, Pablo handed me a pristine sheer cotton batiste handkerchief from his breast pocket to wipe my mouth and my brow. I held the cloth to my lips and panted into it, trying to breathe in some carbon dioxide and get my breathing under control.

"So, what do you say, Gringo? What do you think about coming to work with me?"

I frowned, partially because I was still panting heavily, and partially to indicate I had questions, but mostly at the name he had just called me.

Pablo laughed. "You know 'gringo' is not a derogatory term. It means only that you are not Spanish."

I gave myself a couple of seconds to let that sink in. "Pablo, if we do this"—breath—"if I come to work with you"—breath—"what will Alvaro do?"

"To you?"

"Ah. Yes"—breath—"to me."

"Nothing. I am sending Javier home to Alvaro, and he will deliver a message to him from me. You will never have trouble from Alvaro again."

I felt myself on the edge of once again being able to take a deep breath, until Pablo added, "Unless, you know, he is much madder than even I believe him to be..."

36

I FELT LIKE... WHAT? Not a kid on Christmas morning. A kid on Christmas morning is happy, of course, but he knows he's got only an hour or so, depending on the wherewithal and generosity of his parents, to tear open packages containing new things—two or ten or twenty presents—and he'll like the contents of some, love the contents of one or two, and those he likes or loves will suffice to counteract the disappointment he feels about the rest. In other words, the ecstasy of Christmas morning is conditional, and short-lived, and even a kid knows it.

I felt like a young man on the day after he has graduated from college, relaxed and loose, all his life before him, not knowing what was coming but not intimidated by whatever lay ahead, proud of having met a rigorous goal and turning to divine the next milestone with riotous self-confidence. Part of the reason for my buoyant attitude was the easy solidarity Pablo had offered to me when I told him Alvaro was not the only person who was causing me problems at the moment. There was also Abe—and what Abe was demanding I provide to him in order that I could keep my little laundry business afloat. I told Pablo everything, and then he poured himself another splash of Armagnac and sat back, looking over his lush gardens, while he contemplated my difficulty. "I suggest then," he said, a smile pulling at the corners of his mouth, "we give this Abe exactly what he wants."

Now I walked behind Pablo and Abe, down the wide and glorious mile-long Paseo de Montejo, paying only vague attention to what Pablo was saying, drawing Abe's attention to this piece of architectural interest or that point of historical importance. The Paseo de Montejo has been rightly described as Mérida's Champs Elysees, so Pablo—the ultimate salesman from whom even I could take lessons—was reveling in a richness of topics for conversation. I had told Pablo that, knowing Abe, the beautiful museums along the magnificent, shady street would hold no fascination for our guest; stick to talking about how many times you've been invited by the owners to have dinner at the glorious

Caseo Museo Montes—a museum, yes, and yet still a private home—or the cost of the renovations of this other hacienda, a figure he would have no way of knowing but that he would invent because, of course, Abe was told that he and I had been responsible for the work. I didn't pay strict attention to the tales Pablo was spinning because there was no need. Abe was riveted, and impressed, hungry to eat up whatever the charming Pablo fed him.

Instead, I watched the two of them walk, a few paces ahead of me, Abe waddling along in the mint-colored jacket he couldn't quite button over his bulging belly, a piece of clothing that looked as if it had been borrowed from a refugee of a 1980s country club, and Pablo gliding down the sidewalk, his signature white linen blazer draped over his shoulders. I marveled anew at how, upon Pablo's trim frame, white linen did not seem to wilt in the humid heat of my beloved Mérida.

In any case, by the time we reached Mérida there was very little reason to be concerned about anything that Pablo might have to say to Abe; Abe was completely under his spell. As we'd driven from the airport, after picking Abe up in Pablo's Escalade, we'd passed resort after resort, all virtually the same—big, new buildings, each room with an ocean view, within a complex that included banquet halls, tennis courts and golf courses, all at the end of another palm-lined driveway; each resort overflowing with fat Americans who'd opted for the "all inclusive"—all the food and drink they desired to pacify gaudy appetites that were never quenched. Cameras around pudgy necks, enormous straw handbags slung over the drooping, bronzed skin of forearms, they lined up to board brightly painted, open-air buses to go off on day trips to ogle the quaint huts of the natives and snap pictures of themselves posing before Mayan ruins for the folks back home. And Pablo had intimated carefully, never actually boldly lying, that he and I had built so many of these resorts—that is, the ones we did not own outright. As Abe strained to look out the car's windows at each new passing marvel, almost drooling at the cheap splendor of it all, the phrase 'gullible little peasant' kept echoing in my mind. Abe's tour of Mérida was an absolute tour de force; though, in truth, Pablo's star-making performance, with me as director, had begun before we'd even left the airport.

"Call your friends in customs," I'd told Pablo before Abe arrived, "with your business, you must have some. Have them detain Abe. When he gets off the plane, have them search his bags, his documents, and do it aggressively. Have them accuse him of... I don't know… smuggling, trying to enter the country illegally, whatever they think is plausible."

Pablo had nodded at me. "If that's what you want. I thought we were trying to impress this American friend of yours?"

"He's no friend, Pablo, but he's going to be a whole lot friendlier when you resolve his problem getting through customs."

Pablo had raised an eyebrow at me, and smiled.

He and I watched from the glass-enclosed passenger pick-up area at the airport as Abe's Aeromexico flight arrived. The passengers deplaned, a few harried businessmen along with the usual chubby, ugly Americans, Abe, and— Holy fuck. I squinted out onto the tarmac. With Abe—was that who I thought it was?

I watched, horrified, as two security trucks, yellow and blue lights flashing from their roofs, squealed up to where Abe was walking and six armed customs agents surrounded him, gripping his arms, forcing him onto the tarmac, one guard prodding Abe in his oversized gut with the butt of his rifle. And Charlotte—sweet, angel Charlotte— watching our ruse go down with a gaping mouth, one delicate hand held over her fast-beating heart.

"Stop them, Pablo." I poked the elegant Pablo with my elbow. "Call your men off."

"But, Clint"—Pablo smiled—"you wanted to give Abe a harrowing experience, and my men have only just begun!"

I saw Charlotte bring that small, delightful hand to her mouth, stifle a sob. "Please, Pablo, call them off—now!"

Pablo shook his head, but he stood immediately and pushed open the glass doors that led to the tarmac. "What are you doing to this man?" he shouted as he approached the shake-down in progress. "This man is my business partner and I take offense that he is receiving such a poor welcome to our country!"

The armed guards, off script now too, backed off, and one of them sputtered, "Sorry, Mr. Navarro, we are only doing—"

"Your job, I know," Pablo said quickly, cutting him off before the hapless actor could add, "what you told us to do." Pablo waved them away, took Abe's arm and led him to the building. "Abe Cohen, I am so glad to meet you. Come inside, it is cooler inside, of course, and your friend Clint is here with me..."

Right there with him, in fact—I'd rushed to the tarmac directly behind him. I had the lovely Charlotte's pale, soft hand in mine, patting it to calm her.

Abe's madras shirt was soaked through with sweat, his mint green jacket retrieved from where it had been flung during his 'arrest' now rumpled under an arm, and he was panting from both fear and the heat. "Clint," he said, "I can't believe I'm glad to see you," as his recent tormentors scrambled to obey Pablo's barked orders: "Find Mr. Cohen's luggage and put it in the trunk of my car!"

"Clint, Pablo, this is Charlotte," Abe said off-handedly as he limped into the cool air of the terminal.

"Charlotte Cruet," she offered.

"Delighted to meet you." Pablo turned to offer her his hand in greeting.

"Yes," I said, "delighted."

Charlotte smiled at me, and winked at our secret.

37

CHARLOTTE STROLLED WITH me now, behind Pablo and Abe, keeping their leisurely pace. The day was as humid as Mérida's afternoons ever are; Charlotte's face and neck were glowing and damp, and as we walked I caught her faint smell of roses and fresh-cut pine with each hot breeze.

The first time we'd met, in David and Candace's kitchen, I had not made it past Charlotte's aura—or the red cape her father had handed me!—to remember what she might have been wearing. Today I noted her decidedly upscale yellow silk shift and the Hermes scarf around her neck. "You look... stunning."

Charlotte brushed off my compliment. "Abe sent me to Saks before we left to come down here this morning. He told me to get something for myself to wear, something that looked professional. He didn't want me getting off the plane in my usual cotton slacks and button-down and having to introduce me as his secretary—he didn't want me to make a fool of him."

"Hardly your fault if that happens," I replied and Charlotte, truly a professional, only smiled. "How did your family meet the Cohens?" I asked, to change the subject. "You tell me your Cohen story and I'll tell you mine..."

Charlotte's smile broadened, whether at the thought of the family we both loved or at my double entendre, I couldn't be sure. "We know them from way back. Long enough that I've known them all my life."

I frowned. "I've known them all my life, too—odd that we've never met before the other night..."

She chuckled, not particularly amused. "My parents came to this country in the 1980s, part of the Mariel boatlift. Daddy was a landscape architect in Cuba. In America he became a gardener. One of his first jobs was mowing the grass at David and Candace's—that's how he met David and David helped him get the fifty thousand dollars he'd managed to smuggle out of Cuba into an American bank. You know, helped him open a bank account, and get a credit rating, and finance our house." She shrugged. "You and Jack and Abe didn't exactly hang out with the help's kids."

I was wounded, and I sputtered a defense: "I was the kid of the help, too, you know."

Charlotte merely shrugged again. "Anyway, I was a good ten years younger than you boys. Of course you didn't notice me back then," she added to soften the blow.

She grew quiet then, allowing me to flounder in the awkwardness.

"So, you're in college," I said. "What are you studying?"

Her face brightened, and she turned it once again to me. "To be a teacher. I have younger brothers, and"—she was so excited she'd added her hands to the conversation—"I'm the first one in the family to speak English as my first language, so I was always drafted to help them with their homework, especially language arts, of course—and I loved it! It was my favorite part of the day, you know? Doing homework with my brothers. I graduated, I guess you could say, to helping my parents perfect their English, and, later, I volunteered to teach ESL classes at—"

Her enthusiasm had grown so animated that I had to laugh.

"Don't make fun of me."

"I'm not!" I assured her. "I'm just, you

know, *delighted*. You probably don't know this about me, but I'm in the process right now of building a school to help Mayan kids learn English. It's being built as we speak! I can't wait to get all the financial planning done for this pack of goons so I can make it my own priority again and not just the contractor's."

Charlotte laughed with me. "What do you know about running a school?" She used both hands to pull her hair to the back of her head. She gathered up stray strands that were shining in the sunlight, smoothed them down and tied the whole lustrous bundle back with a hair tie she'd been wearing around her wrist. "How will you decide on the curriculum, and set policy, and find teachers?"

"Well," I admitted, "there are some details I still have to work out."

She'd raised the exact concerns that I'd placed at the back of my mind, at least while I worked out my current banking adventures, but I knew she was right and I'd have to address these critical issues soon— at least start advertising for teachers and combing through résumés.

But I didn't have to think about those problems at this precise moment in time. Right now I could enjoy strolling along a wide, shady avenue in the company of a genuinely relaxed beauty, and let myself fall into the fantasy my Charlotte-fevered brain was concocting: she would find her life's work with me in Mérida, move here and take over creating the curricula for my school, hiring and supervising the teachers we would employ and, eventually, she would discover that she loved me, too, and would move into my house and, together, we would create a home as relaxed and beautiful as she was.

And Abe? Well! Even a cursory look at the damage he had caused for my new bank showed that he'd personally approved over seventy million in fraudulent loans—an excellent reason to fire his sorry ass, and I was sure that, even if David and Candace wouldn't proactively cast out their own son, I could lobby the votes I needed from among the other shareholders to get the job done. Perfect love and perfect revenge: it was a brilliant daydream.

But I didn't want to waste a moment more of my time in Charlotte's company in a daydream. I wanted to suck up every molecule of her scent, every second of her smile. I was about to suggest that we all head to Ki Xocolatl, sit in their garden courtyard and have an iced coffee, sample their white chocolates shaped liked ears of corn, and their pink peppercorn dark chocolate bites, when Pablo's cell phone began to ring.

He excused himself, walked a few more paces ahead of all of us, and reached into the pocket of his still-pristine white blazer, frowning as he checked the caller ID, touching the green button to answer the call, putting the phone to his ear. "Yes?"

The sky over our small village was Arctic blue, no trace of a cloud or storm. An ocean breeze careened across the boulevard, blowing tiny sand devils around us. It was late on a typical sultry afternoon, dampness was everywhere, and it was peaceful, but, typical of the tropics, a storm could always roar up in mere hours.

Pablo ended his phone call and quickly punched in another. He barked some orders into the phone that he was just far enough away for any of us to hear, and slid it back into his pocket. He paused for just a moment before turning back to us. "My dear new friends," he said to Charlotte and Abe, "you must forgive us. Clint and I have been called to a meeting. If you will go in here where it is cool"—he ushered them into the door of the very chocolate shop where I'd been hoping to sit with Charlotte—"my driver will be here in five minutes to take you back to Clint's home. You may, of course, stay here as long as you like—you should try their chocolates, very delicious. Simply tell my driver your pleasure, he is at your disposal. Clint"—he turned to me and took my arm, pulling me away from Charlotte and down the block toward the lot where he'd parked his Escalade, at a pace I had to struggle to match—"you and I have much to discuss."

"Sure, Pablo," I told him. "Of course." At the lot he beeped open the doors and practically shoved me toward the passenger side. "What the hell is going on?"

Pablo seated himself behind the steering wheel, adjusted his seatbelt and took another moment to process whatever news he had just received before he let me in on it.

"Javier," Pablo said at last.

"What about him?"

"He's dead."

38

CHANCE HAD LONG been my best friend. Chance had been the reason I'd vacationed in this particular town in Mexico, fallen in love with the place and moved here. Chance had been the reason I met and fell deeply I love with a Mayan young man. Someone I could not live without. Someone who had much to teach me about being happy and content—lessons I was but beginning to learn before Chance once again intervened. Chance had placed me at one particular election victory party, put me in the position to meet Alvaro and make four million bucks, and then put me in front of Pablo and the new opportunity to launder money not for one measly and minor drug dealer, but for the biggest in the whole country. Chance and I, when you took the long view, went a lot farther back than that; chance was involved right up to its ears in my mother's answering an ad in a long-ago newspaper to go to work keeping Candace Cohen's house. It was a job that had given me entrée to a group of good people and an entire way of life that likely would have been wholly foreign to me if Mom had gone to work for anyone else.

It might seem that chance had recently decided to thumb its nose at me, but I wasn't about to start mistrusting it now, not after it had been such a staunch ally in my life.

"How?" I asked Pablo. "How is Javier dead?"

We'd arrived at Pablo's splendid hacienda, arranged ourselves on his patio, over the glasses of cold white wine his maid had served to us before Pablo decided to answer my question.

"Alvaro," Pablo said.

It was a verdict I had feared but would not let myself believe until Pablo said it. "He killed his own brother-in-law?"

"*Had* him killed, I suspect."

I shook my head, trying to make sense of what I now knew. "His wife? She must be devastated."

"I am told she has left Alvaro's house and gone to her mother's." He added, with a shrug, "She apparently tried to stab him with a kitchen knife when she found out her brother was dead. Some of Alvaro's men have gone with her, to protect her mother's house, they are so fearful of what else Alvaro might do."

"But... *why?*"

Pablo shrugged again. "He disappointed Alvaro. He did not succeed in killing you."

I kept myself from gasping only with a herculean effort. Pablo picked up his glass of wine, carefully, by the stem of the tall glass, and let the light reflect its green-golden color before lifting it to his mouth to take a sip. "Our way of life"—he twirled the liquid in his glass as he spoke—"is too rich for you?"

I frowned. Was it? Could I handle the danger, and the loss, inherent in it? A few weeks ago I would have spoken thoughtlessly, said that of course I could manage any circumstance if four million dollars was sitting at the end of it. I would have said that I craved the adrenaline rush of being shot at. And then I actually was. That Alvaro was almost certainly a murderer was somehow acceptable to me, in the abstract; now I had known one of his victims, a real, living person who was no longer living because of Alvaro.

I spoke carefully. "I'm not naïve, Pablo, but I admit I'm shocked. I suppose, in every business, a boss has the right to fire the employees who aren't performing up to level...

But when the boss is... unbalanced... I did nothing that should have caused Alvaro to want to fire me, so sending Javier to... come after me. To get rid of him when he failed to get rid of me... This is not good company policy."

Pablo smiled at my coy metaphors. "No. It is not." He raised his glass to take another sip of his wine. "You should try this. It is very good, and it is only growing warm sitting there untouched."

I did as I was told. The wine truly was exceptional, and I wished I could have savored it, but I was slightly preoccupied.

"Clint," Pablo said as I swallowed hard to push down the delicious wine, "I have many, many friends. We have, among us, several million dollars—" He paused, to calculate, and revised his statement—"Several hundred million dollars each month or so that we would like to protect."

I gulped another swallow of wine. It went down easier this time.

"I have seen what you have done for Alvaro, and I know a little about your new banking arrangements in the United States. I think you will be the one who can help us to protect our assets. Now"—Pablo held up a warning finger—"we are not going to give you twenty percent of our money. Between the two of us, I think Alvaro was rash to offer you such a large cut, though he did offer it and his regret is no reason to renege on a stupid offer. I will offer you five percent on behalf of myself and my friends. If you do the math you will see that it is quite a generous offer, considering the quantity of dollars we are talking about…"

He paused to let me do the calculations. Even at just one hundred million a month that was five million for me—quite acceptable as steady income.

"So," Pablo continued, "this is the first of the terms you must accept from me if you would like to work with us."

I nodded. "And the other terms?"

Pablo once again shrugged. "You will meet my friends, I think you should, but you will deal only with me. I am the boss, as you say."

After Alvaro's madness, Pablo's sanity seemed intense, and comforting. "I can agree to that."

"And," Pablo held up the warning finger again, "one more thing."

"Yes?"

He swallowed the last of the wine in his glass before he spoke. "You will see, working with me and my friends, that we are not hard men. We are negotiators. We prefer to do business like gentlemen—we are generous in rewarding people for their goodwill, and reasonable about talking people out of their bad ideas." He shrugged. "Bribery and coercion, this is what some people say, but have you ever willingly worked for someone who did not pay you well? Or met a boss who rewarded his employees for their bad judgment?" He took another sip of his wine. "I am not a violent man, Clint. I am always reluctant to terminate the employment of one of my men, though, from time to time, it becomes necessary—"

"I would never do anything to earn your distrust—"

"It is not you I am speaking of," Pablo said. "But I am not sure how much longer I will be content with Alvaro on my payroll."

When I'd stopped reeling, Pablo called to his maid. "I think my guest and I will have a little dinner now, Marta," he said. "And you will make up the blue guest room for him to stay the night, please."

"Oh, no, Pablo, I will love to have dinner with you, but I can't stay the night. I've got Charlotte and Abe at my house—"

"You will stay," he told me. "I have not yet had the opportunity, of course, to talk with Alvaro and I don't know what he might be planning. We must give him time to cool down, and to prove himself. For now, you will stay, for your protection."

"Good god, man," I shouted, totally losing myself, "you think Alvaro might go to my house to do me harm? Charlotte and Abe are there!"

Pablo frowned at me. "You care about this?"

Well, I thought, not about Abe so much, though if he ended up slaughtered at my house I would have a hard time explaining that to Candace and David. They were not Abe's foremost fans, but I was sure they did not actually want him dead. As for Charlotte, if anything happened to her, I might just die myself in response.

"Pablo! Please!"

"Fine, fine." Pablo called to his maid again. "Marta, send Cristobal in here."

"Cristobal?"

"My man. He will go to your house, tell your guests that you and I have been called out of the city for this important meeting we are attending. He will take them to the airport and put them on my plane to take them back to Miami. Will this suit you?"

I put my head in my hands. "Yes, Pablo. Thank you. Do it now, please. Have him do it right now."

39

PABLO HAD ARRANGED the meeting to take place in a small pueblo on the south side on the Gulf of Mexico, Chuburna, far away from the busy goings on in Mérida, where the avenues and the buildings that lined them were fine and stately, testaments to the grandness of a bygone era. Chuburna by contrast, had been a fishing village for more than a thousand years. At one time five thousand people had lived there, when the temple that lay about a mile inland had been built, which was in the third century BC, as far as the educated had guessed. Now there were fewer than three hundred Mayans who called the place home. For all its distance from its sacred past, the village retained a certain otherworldly serenity, embodied by its inhabitants who moved with calm purpose through their daily routines—catching

fish for that day's meal from their pole-pro-
pelled boats, or taking the odd tourist out
to fish for himself on the blue-green waters
of the lagoon that bordered its western side.
The air smelled of fish and salt, the white
sand beach was glass-littered, and herons,
egrets, and eagles were as at home there as
the people.

The basic mode of transportation in the
village was by foot, augmented by a bicycle
or two. Our motorcade of fancy cars turned
heads, and when we turned inland toward
the temple itself, the rutted road was lined,
every fifty feet or so, with a pair of armed
guards wearing police uniforms, though it
wasn't clear that they were actually police.
The villagers, simple and rural and agrari-
an people, were savvy enough not to follow
our cars into this line of potential fire. They
averted their eyes and returned to their
tasks, cutting the heads off the daily catch
and tossing them back in the water to lure
tomorrow's harvest.

Our cars rocked over the even more deeply
rutted road, headed inland. The temple was
deep within the rain forest, and it belonged,
every ancient stone of it, to Pablo. He had
spent, he'd explained to me, somewhere in
the neighborhood of thirty-five million, give or
take a million here and there, restoring and

fortifying the national historic treasure and, in exchange for assuring that Mexico would not lose a structure so significant to its country's heritage, the country had, in essence, gifted it to him—and to his heirs—for their private use; it would never be opened to the public. Pablo's only obligation was to maintain, in unspoiled and historically accurate condition, the edifice. He took this obligation seriously. As we approached, several dozen small, dark-skinned, round-faced Mayans clung to the sides of the temple, dangling from ropes secured from ever higher levels of the structure, using paint brushes to clean the stones. They worked in this way, Pablo told me, in teams and year-round, because constant maintenance was required to keep the tropical rot at bay—indeed, the majority of the village's population worked for him at some point over the course of a year. None of the Mayans, however, would work *inside* the temple. This was because certain rooms of the temple were tombs, and the villagers believed their ancestors still resided within, that it was these corpses that would return to life when the Mayan calendar—and the world as we knew it—came to an end.

I hadn't been sure what to expect when Pablo had told me the meeting was going to take place at his "camp"—some place rural and rustic, certainly—but that the "camp" turned out to be a restored Mayan temple seemed both supremely eccentric and weirdly appropriate. But I didn't yet know the half of it.

I noticed what appeared to be a series of squat, metal, industrial structures mostly obscured behind the temple. "My power plant," Pablo told me. "It services my camp, and a few of the homes in the village as well, though I'm hoping I can bring electricity to the entire village with time. Some of the elders are resistant. They've lived their whole lives without electricity and do not see its purpose—"

"Your power plant?" I was blown away and didn't even attempt to hide my incredulity.

"Powered by a solar field about a quarter mile further west. You can hike out there, if you'd like, to see it. It's really very striking—I was careful to preserve the area around it as a thing of natural beauty when I built it—" He opened his arms for me to go into the temple before him. "After you."

Inside the temple, the dark dampness was somewhat relieved by torches Pablo's minions had lit prior to our arrival. They now burned brightly in sconces high on the walls.

"Think of this as my foyer." Pablo laughed, leading the way through the echoing central space. "Below us?" he drew my attention to the floor with another open-armed gesture.

"Below the ground?"

"Yes. Machine guns, shoulder-fired missiles, twelve thousand rounds of ammunition—the most secure armory, either private and public, I believe, in the country because, of course, my government would never destroy such a sacred treasure as this building, which they would surely have to do to relieve me of my firearms. And they know this."

Pablo pulled from the breast pocket of his blazer what looked like an ordinary stamped silver key fob and, when we'd walked to the other side of the large, central space, through a narrow stone passageway, he pressed one of the icons stamped onto its face. The stone wall at the back of the niche rumbled for a brief moment, then began to roll away, receding into the wall to its right like a pocket door. Pablo crooked his finger for me to follow him into the tunnel that opened up to us.

The tunnel, ten-feet wide and stone-paved, meandered on a downward slope beneath the limestone terrain, emerging three thousand feet later into a ten-thousand-square-foot, concrete-walled inner sanctum. Half a dozen men, all seemingly engrossed in tasks being performed on their computer monitors, worked at two banks of long glass tables in the middle of the room. A lone man sat before a wall monitoring a grid of six sixty-inch flat screen TV monitors that beamed twenty-four-hour live satellite views of the two square miles surrounding Pablo's camp as well as the activity at various points of the Mexican-U,S. border, and at several airport terminals, including Mérida and Miami, but encompassing smaller facilities as well, including a few that looked like only landing strips in the jungle. Or, I peered more closely, was that the Everglades?

"I need to be prepared for any assault on my livelihood," Pablo said, an arm sweeping past the technology, the other holding the watch fob. He pressed a different icon now and a panel in the back wall began to rumble and slide away. This passage, wider but much shorter, and paneled in rich, chocolate mahogany, led directly into a luxurious, circular living space—more deep mahogany on the walls, doors set at intervals in between pillars of rose-colored marble, beneath a mahogany catwalk from which one could access the second story of a two-story library, furnished with plush, wine-colored leather sofas and loveseats. There were no windows, of course—I suspected we were at least two stories beneath the ground—but the room was washed in the most pleasing, natural-looking ambient light.

"That door will take you to the kitchen, and that one to the dining room. These doors"—another sweep of his arm—"are to guest rooms—I will assign one to you later. And the ceiling?" He twirled a finger to indicate I was to look above me. "Lined with lead. We are completely undetectable! You will, however, be able to use your cell phone after its been adjusted—leave it on the table there"—he indicated a Louis XIV library table that I thought was rather more authentic than merely a stylish reproduction—"and I'll have one of the tech fellows deal with it before we go to our rooms to get ready for dinner."

I couldn't decide whether I was more reluctant to give up my phone so Pablo's tech people could toy with it, or to be without any way to communicate with anyone outside of this luxurious and lovely tomb for the duration of the summit—or, now that Pablo had mentioned food, if I was simply distracted by the aromas coming from the kitchen.

"My chef has been here all day, working on our dinner. He insists even more than I do that my guests will have a feast—which is why he has kept his job for nearly fourteen years now. Boeuf bourguignon this evening—I love French food, and I am a traditionalist, I fear."

I grinned. "I have a friend in Florida who's the same way," I said. "Named Xavier. You ought to meet him sometime."

"Perhaps I will, Clint. You never know."

I took my currently-worthless cell phone out of my pocket and dropped it on the library table. "All very James Bond, what you've got going on down here, Pablo."

Pablo laughed. "I have never heard of James Bond having to deal with temperamental stone masons, or a septic tank backing up forty feet below ground. Will you have a drink with me, before the others arrive?"

"Scotch?"

"Fine choice—"

40

I WAS GOING TO have to employ some fancy mnemonic devices to keep all their names straight, these new potential partners of mine—Luis and Lucas, Mateo and Matias, Tomas and Andres, Emiliano and Felipe and Joaquin—sixteen altogether, drug kingpins and a few of their more important *sub-contractors*, though they could have been a gathering of prosperous businessmen from any industry the world over. All except, of course, Alvaro who, in the company of these older and surprisingly distinguished men, looked—and acted—like a prosperous rock star on a bender. He greeted his associates as an equal—even the refined Pablo—with a sort of jolliness that could be understood as confidence but never mistaken for sincerity. He did not greet me at all, keeping his distance, glowering at me through narrowed eyes from across the room or across the dinner table.

With our bellies full of French food and wine, we left our seats at the massive Tudor-era-looking table in the dining room and retreated back to the library where Pablo passed out Cuban cigars and heavy lead crystal glasses of brandy. When each man had his drink in hand, and those who were smoking had lit their cigars—the aroma of them merely teasing our noses before the smoke and odor were swept from the room by way of Pablo's state-of-the-art air filtration system—Pablo raised his glass.

"I am keeping my promise, gentlemen! We will not talk business tonight! Tonight is for feasting, and for conversation among ourselves, and tomorrow we will talk of why I have asked you all here with me. Tonight I want only to toast you who have traveled from all corners of our country to be here— and I toast our guest of honor, Mr. Clint Kennedy." He pointed his glass in my direction and I responded to the scattered applause this gesture stirred by lifting my glass a bit higher. "To Mister Clint Kennedy, who has a solution to a problem that has bedeviled every one of us!"

Alvaro shot me a look from across the opulent room, where he slouched against one of the rose marble pillars. I knew exactly what he was thinking: the bank scheme that he knew I was going to present to his fellow drug lords in the morning had been *his* idea; he'd been the one to discover my banking connections in the U.S. and seek me out to propose the deal, and now I was the one getting credit for it among his peers. I was the one who stood to profit handsomely from his brainchild. None of which was true, of course. Sure, he'd sought out an American banker and told me his tale of woe—all those woefully unuseable millions—but without me they would still be sitting and collecting dust in his guest room. I turned my head so I didn't have to look at him glaring at me with his hard eyes. I would have been willing to admit his part in the creation of my new business, but his part went only so far. A man may come up to his friend and say, "I think it would be a good idea to make a way to fasten papers together with a piece of metal," and the friend may then go to a tooling shop to invest his time and money in working with a machinist to create a prototype, but when the prototype proves successful the man doesn't get credit for inventing the paperclip.

I let Alvaro avoid me. Instead, I talked with Luis about the proper technique for restoring frescos—he had just bought a dilapidated Colonial in Mexico City and Pablo had told him I had recently been through my own restoration and had done a magnificent job of it. I talked with Tomas and Felipe about my school—and Felipe was so moved he told me that, if ever I found myself in need of a patron for it, to call upon him: "This is good work you are doing, Clint, and I would love to be part of it, if you ever have reason to want me." I talked at length with Andres about the relative merits of this tequila over that other one—and we ended up with Pablo, at the library's well-stocked bar, taste testing. I confess to a bit of astonishment at my company; this was certainly not how, in my ignorance, I would ever have envisioned an evening with Mexican drug lords might turn out. These men were rivals, of course, but respectful of each other's territory, and acumen; men of substance and taste, and wildly interesting as individuals. My evening with the drug dealers was turning out to be pleasant, profitable, and fun.

Alvaro grew more agitated as each hour passed, as he witnessed each new example of how I was being not merely accepted by the people he considered his peers but beginning to experience a genuine camaraderie with them—talking more loudly, walking with more macho, gesturing with more force, including keeping up a beat on the ornate library table as he fought to sustain Lucas's attention on whatever it was they were talking about over there, pounding the table as if it were a bongo drum and shifting his weight from foot to foot as if he might break into a dance.

And, eventually, to my real sorrow, he did.

He started to pull the pairs of gilt chairs that flanked the marble pillars into a semi-circle, urging a reluctant audience to have a seat, attempting to direct all attention to himself, beginning the full-out boogie of the bull dance: "You have to anger the bull! You have to make your opponent *mad*! If you don't infuriate him, he won't charge at you with the death run!" Alvaro was twirling, spinning an imaginary cape over his head, narrowly bending out of the way of the non-existent bull and then, to my horror, he began to snort and tamp his right foot. He raised his hands to his forehead, forefingers extended to simulate horns and, thus, charged at Luis, drawing short to charge at Tomas, and then at Emiliano...

I watched the display in fascinated shock—the men not even pretending to be amused, Alvaro without even the slightest clue that he was making a drunken ass of himself.

The first time I had seen Alvaro do the bull dance had been on election night, what... less than a few weeks before? His graceful movement had impressed me then, as had his way of holding an audience rapt. But the audience that night had been adoring bullfighting fans and, in my defense, it was the first time I'd seen him perform it. And the bull metaphor itself went only so far—and required the speaker to tailor it to his listeners. To know enough to stop regaling onlookers who were clearly disdainful.

I had rarely borne witness to such efforts, or seen someone so pathetically out of his element trying to lay claim to its leadership. I had enough residual respect for what I'd seen him do when facing down an actual bull to look away.

41

THE NEXT MORNING the library table had been stripped of its decoration—two silver candelabra and several leather-bound first editions and, sadly, a mounted rhinoceros horn—and laid with crisp, white linen. On top were an urn brewing aromatic Brazilian coffee, a bone china bowl and pitcher filled with sugar and cream, platters of flakey pastries.

"Good morning! Good morning!" Pablo was an early riser, heartiest in the mornings, and welcomed his guests with gusto. "Try the danish!"

In contrast, Alvaro, one of the last to arrive, slunk into the room, his usually lustrous black hair stringy, his complexion wan, bags under his eyes, proving that even beautiful rock stars were no match for the effects of too much wine and brandy and too little sleep. He stumbled to the library table, poured a cup of coffee for himself with a trembling hand, and retreated to perch on one of the gilt chairs under the library catwalk.

I had dressed in the new, dove gray Armani three-piece suit I'd brought for the occasion, a silk, ice blue tie around my neck, and I knew I looked the part of someone who could address the problem that, as Pablo had prepped me, was an immediate concern for all of those gathered here. I owned up to myself, however, that I was feeling just a little nervous about what I was going to say to these men when Pablo started the meeting and turned the floor over to me. Ever since I was a kid, I'd been a natural closer, *one-on-one*; speaking to a group had always made my biochemicals kick into overdrive. I relished the faint tingle of fear, and rehearsed my prepared remarks again in my head while I sipped my coffee.

Pablo called the gathering to order—"Gentlemen! Gentlemen!"—tapping his coffee cup with his silver spoon, and began with some general comments while everyone found a comfortable seat on the leather sofas. "We have all seen the news reports of drug and gang violence in the border cities of our country. Ciudad Juarez is one of the worst hit and the reason is obvious: it is one of the principal routes we use for getting our wares across the border. Gentlemen, here in this room, we all work together. In that spirit, I ask you to speak with your men down the line, to infuse them with the same sense of cooperation. I remind you: when the death toll rises too high, the government declares another war on our business venture, and no one likes to have that expense."

There was genuine applause for Pablo's appeal, and even a few robust cries of "Si, Si!"

"Second," Pablo continued," as we all know, one of our costliest line items is pay-offs to the border agents—our own govern-ment is not the only one to engage in warfare with us from time to time! In the U.S., my intelligence tells me, there is fresh appetite for another battle or two..." There were a few grunts from Pablo's audience, and more than a few heavy sighs. "I am not saying it has to be done immediately, but I do think we will need to give the Americans another border bust sooner than later. We must keep them believing that they are getting ahead in our little war, yes?"

He waited for his fellows to reply, as if the question wasn't rhetorical. A chorus of reluctant "Si, si," was returned to him, and he clapped his hands once to show he was pleased. "I know it is not the most pleasant part of doing business, but we do need to keep the enemy engaged. What would it do to our whole business model if we gave them time to sit back and think and realize the inevitable solution to our war games—as well as to so many of their internal problems—is to simply legalize drugs, collect the taxes on them, and stop paying for the prison space necessary to house all the teenagers they bust for having a ten-dollar bag of marijuana in their pocket!"

During the laughter that followed his comment, Pablo gestured to me to join him in the center of the room. I thought, as I walked to his side, what a thrill it is to be alive, and on the very verge of being scandalously prosperous. On the cusp of becoming a world-class philanthropist. I imagined the looks that would cross David's face when I regaled him with the details of each new accomplishment.

"Gentlemen, you have all met my friend Clint Kennedy—we had a lovely evening with him last night, did we not?" My eyes moved automatically to Alvaro as this question was asked, but he was slump-shouldered and staring, squinty-eyed, into the depths of his coffee cup.

"My friend, Clint Kennedy," Pablo repeated, emphasizing the word "friend", "has exciting news for us, and I will let him talk in just a moment, but first I want to tell you a little bit about why he is here. We all know, of course, that of the currencies in circulation in the world, the United States's is the most stable—"

There were a few chuckles around the room.

"Hard to believe, I know, when you consider all their war debt and their failing banks, but it's nonetheless true. Well, my friend Clint owns a bank in the United States—"

I could not resist a glance at Alvaro at this—as I'd suspected, this news made him open his eyes in surprise.

"And not just a bank, gentlemen, a *solvent* bank with many, many branches and all the time acquiring more branches—"

The room broke into applause at this, most of it coming directly on the heels of the word "solvent."

"And he has figured out a way to get our money into his bank!"

This exclamation was cause for some amusement—laughter and some catcalls, mostly good-natured, from men who were not unaccustomed to crooks coming to call: "I'll bet he has!" "Yes, but how will *I* get it back out?" "How do we know we can trust him?" "We will show him what happens when we do not trust him!" That sort of thing. Not a word from Alvaro, just that long stare, then back into his coffee cup. I'd hazarded a look.

"Gentlemen," Pablo offered, "I am trusting him with my money. I hope my endorsement might persuade you of my friend's reliability."

That shut them up.

"For a small consideration—five percent..."

I saw Alvaro's head jerk to attention.

"...plus certain other fees, bank fees, currency exchange, payoffs to appropriate officials, he can arrange to put your money into a stable bank in America, too."

The room grew still with the sound of men thinking. And the sound of one man's blood pressure rising. His heart racing. His brain exploding.

When Pablo added, "I am certain I don't have to persuade you of the benefits of having your money in a sound American financial institution," a sound erupted like the wailing of a large, hungry cat. A large, hungry, wounded cat. A caged, bleeding animal who had always before had teeth and claws and brute strength to rely upon.

Eventually the wail formed itself into words. "*Five percent!* This thief charged me twenty percent! He screwed me out of *my* money with *my* idea for him to put my money into the American bank!"

There was spit flying from Alvaro's mouth

along with his words as he raged, and he was no longer sitting slumped in his gilt chair, he was on his feet, pacing haphazardly among the men, winding his way around chairs and sofas, knocking his flailing arms into the backs of chairs, lamps on the tables, the top of Luis's head. "*Hijo de puta!*"

"*He didn't even tell me it was his bank!*" Alvaro shrieked.

Pablo tried reason. "*Hijo*, you were the one who offered twenty percent, as I understand it. Have I been told something wrong? I don't think I have, and, so, if you make an offer, you must keep your word. I think you did not keep your word?"

"*My* money! *My* idea! I am the one who has earned your five percent, not this fucker!" Alvaro bawled.

Pablo allowed himself a small laugh at this notion. "Alvaro, I think you are taking credit for a fantasy in your head—"

"*My* money! *My* idea," Alvaro insisted, knocking into a small table near Emiliano, setting a porcelain lamp atop it rocking. Emiliano was unable to catch it before it fell to the floor. Pablo gasped as it shattered—I presumed because of its price—and Mateo, who had been sitting next to Emiliano, stood and reached into his pocket, whipped out a Titanium Gold Desert Eagle .44 and cracked Alvaro with it across the back of his head.

The group of us stood over Alvaro, listening to him groan, watching a thin trickle of blood leak out around where he lay on Pablo's carpet.

"Is he all right?" I could barely breathe for all the adrenaline coursing through me.

"He will be." Pablo took his key fob out of his pocket and pressed one of its icons. The door that led out to the control room opened smoothly and one of the men stationed there entered.

"Yes, Señor Navarro?"

Pablo waved a hand at where Alvaro lay. "Get him back to his room, and see that he doesn't bleed all over the place on the way." He waved his finger in a circle at the blood already seeping into the carpet. "And get Berta in here to clean this up."

As Pablo's man grabbed Alvaro under his armpits, hoisted him to his feet and helped him stumble out of the library, the rest of the dealers took up their seats again on the sofas, picked up their cups of coffee, and took bites of their danishes. And then Tomas spoke, his mouth filled with pastry, "Pablo, is there anything to what he says about your friend stealing his money?"

Pablo feigned shock. "Do you think I am so stupid?"

Tomas swallowed. "No, no, no!"

"Of course you do not," Pablo agreed.

42

I LOOSENED MY TIE, slid the knot and stretched my neck. "Jack, I didn't even have to say a word!"

"No chance to practice your sales pitch, huh?"

"Pablo did the selling for me—and Alvaro sealed the deal with his little tantrum." I kicked off my shoes and lay back on the sumptuous feather bed in Pablo's guest room. The bed had been freshly made since I'd rolled out of it this morning—a hallmark, I would learn, of being Pablo's guest: you used a towel, a clean one was folded in its place; you used the glass on your bathroom counter to get a drink of water, it was replaced with a newly polished one; you sat on the bed to tie your shoes, a maid magically appeared the moment you left your room to smooth the duvet.

"I mean," I said to Jack, "I don't think any of them held him in the highest regard to start with so, you know—the enemy of my enemy is my friend, and all that. If Alvaro didn't like me, that was the icing on their cake." I laughed, and then I reminded myself to conduct this conversation with as much dignity as Jack and I could muster between us: Pablo's men had tweaked my cell so that I could use it down here in the bunker and, while it didn't look or sound bugged, you never could tell. I made a mental note to lose the phone as soon as I was above ground again and get a new one that I was sure hadn't been tampered with.

"Yeah, I've got to meet this Pablo—I mean, Abe loves him. *Loves* him, and you know Abe doesn't love no one that ain't Abe. Raving to Mom and Dad about how smart he is, and how sophisticated, and how he must come from a good family to have manners like that, and he even said he'd have to re-evaluate his opinion of you—if someone like Pablo wants to do business with you, you can't be all bad. Shit like that."

"Hell of a thing," I said as I stretched, "when you can't trust a person to hate you on a consistent basis."

"Says you guys kind of gave him the bum's rush out of the country, though?"

I squirmed. I didn't want to get into it over the phone. I didn't yet have a full grasp of the honor code among drug dealers, and there was a murder involved, after all, and, strangely, probably because it was supposed to have been me who ended up dead, I wasn't particularly upset about it. "Don't worry about it. No biggie. I had just had enough of Abe and needed to get rid of him."

"Copy that."

"Speaking of, have you seen Charlotte since they got back?"

"Who?"

"Charlotte—Abe's secretary. Chester's daughter."

"Oh, yeah. No. Where was she?"

"Oh, for Christ's sake, Jack, in Mexico, with Abe."

"Really? That fat fuck sure knows how to milk it, doesn't he? I don't know what he's got her doing up here except ordering him lunch and picking up his dry cleaning. What's he need her for in Mexico?"

I shrugged, scrunching myself deeper into the down pillows behind my head. "Maybe your dad told him to take her with him—he gave her that job to keep an eye on your big brother. Who knows what kind of trouble David worried he'd get into in a foreign country?"

We both had a laugh, Jack stopping short to mutter, "Hey. Charlotte. Are you trying to tap that?"

I rolled my eyes. "I don't think I'd put it quite that way."

Jack cackled. "Clint is sweet on Charlotte!"

"Are you in third grade?" I asked.

"Are you ever going to acknowledge you grew up to be a gay man?" he countered.

I sighed. He and I had been over this before. "I don't give a flying fuck if you want to slap that label on me, happy as hell to have it except it isn't correct—not that it's anyone's business, including yours, who I like to sleep with but, just for the record, I'm bi. *Bi*, Jack, and, based on how I think I'm starting to feel about Charlotte, the other team's winning right now."

"Whatever," Jack said, and I could picture his eyes rolling too right about then.

"I have to go. Lunch is being served in half an hour and that business with Alvaro made me feel crappy and I want a shower before I have to go meet up with everybody again. I just called to put you on notice that we're going to start transferring money again, probably day after tomorrow, so strap yourself in and keep your hands inside the ride."

"Aye, aye, Capitan. I've got to run, too—I'm meeting Sharon for lunch."

"Abe's Sharon?"

"I don't know any other Sharon."

"Update me on the upcoming divorce next time we talk."

"Oh, please, the bank's solvent again. There's not going to be a divorce."

"Then why else does she want to have lunch with you? What else do you two have to talk about?"

Jack paused. "Good point."

43

L UNCH WAS GROUPER prepared *a la plancha,* with a white wine and butter sauce, and an excellent, flinty Pouilly-Fumé, taken around the massive, Tudor-style table in the dining room. Pablo tried to steer the conversation away from business—it was his inclination, both from preference and tradition, to keep the event of breaking bread a purely social one—but the idea of scrubbing their dirty money so that it smelled all fresh and legal, and providing them with consistent, convenient access to piles of it in a secure currency, was far too much of a temptation. And these men had big plans for their newly legitimate and American money—they were going to open convenience stores, buy construction companies, take over all the developments that had gone bust in South Florida and turn them into nursing homes.

Before the maid had finished clearing our plates, we dove into logistics.

"Is there a limit on the amount of cash you can transfer in one day?" Matias asked.

"Yes. Currently I can process eight million a day."

Joaquin frowned. "You're telling me if I give you eight million dollars at nine AM—"

"That I can have it in your U.S. bank account and ready for your use by five PM. Yes, sir, I am," I said and he sat back, calculating how long it would take him to legalize his stash at that rate. I wanted, more than anything in the world at that moment, to know the size of that stash—to be able to calculate my potential profits based on some hard numbers—but I knew better than to ask the question directly at this juncture of the deal and held my tongue.

"So, you take one million from eight of us one day, and a million from eight of us the next day..." Emiliano wondered out loud.

I shook my head. "That's not, actually, the most practical approach. You're located all across the country, and we have to physically transport the money to my Mexican bank in order for them to process the transaction. That means the bank sends an armored truck to pick up your cash and it will be more efficient to have them pick up a whole day's transfer limit at one location at a time. At least it will be for the time being. As Pablo told you, I'm currently acquiring more branches in the U.S. and that will speed things up."

Note to self: talk to Juan Carlos about the possibility of using his bank's local branches in various locations across Mexico and/or ramping up his staff in Mérida to increase his transfer capabilities. Also: talk with David, and with Pablo—in that order—about the possibility of picking up American drug profits directly in America; no need to transport it across the border twice as I assumed was currently the case. Of course I said nothing about these concerns to the partners gathered around the table; they were already salivating at what I had put on their plates and I saw no need to go into detail about how I made my sausage.

The maid returned then, bearing coffee. We fell silent as she served us, though I expected, working here, she had been privy to any number of confidential conversations and Pablo trusted her entirely. The Mexican government had long tried to enlist its citizens in fighting the cartels, but it simply wasn't human nature to fight an entity that provided you with a good living and, in Chuburna, the population was thriving because Pablo conducted his business there.

Luis added cream and an alarming amount of sugar to his small china cup of brew and stirred until it had dissolved and the maid had once again returned to the kitchen. "What you are telling us is that we must go one at a time. And, therefore, some of us will have to wait over two weeks in order to even begin transforming our money."

That was a downside, and I admitted it with a nod.

Mateo slapped the table, a way of drawing our attention. "Then, in that case, we will have a lottery. We will draw names to see in what order we will give our friend Clint our money."

"And rotate through the order every sixteen—excuse me, seventeen—days?" Tomas asked.

"Ah, account for the weekends," I hastened to add. "The banks have limited hours on Saturdays, and they're closed completely on Sundays."

"And, of course, Pablo, you are exempt from the lottery. You must have your turn first, in gratitude for bringing us this opportunity," Joaquin added, and the others around the table voiced their agreement, though Pablo himself deferred.

"I appreciate your kindness, gentlemen," he said, "but we are in this together, as in all things. I am happy to take my place among you."

The strategy of his graciousness was not lost on me. Taking his turn in a lottery would cost Pablo very little, in the short term; in the long term, he would have one more favor to call in, as necessary. I thought, not for the first time, how much I was going to learn from this man.

44

PABLO HAD PROVIDED a silver-plated, Tiffany's champagne bucket from which to draw the scraps of paper—torn sheets of Pablo's watermarked stationary bearing each dealer's name written with the Waterman fountain pens Pablo had passed out to each man as if they were Bics. Pablo drew an honest third place in the lottery and, satisfied with our afternoon's business, suggested we retreat once again to our rooms to relax before dinner. His chef was preparing Cassoulet for us that evening, a heavy meal, and we would need to restore ourselves to enjoy it properly.

The after-lunch coffee had done little to counter the effects of the three glasses of Pouilly-Fumé I'd enjoyed with my fish. A little nap to sleep off the wine would be the smart thing to do for my weary body, but I doubted I could turn off my brain. It was vibrating with anticipation, thoughts bouncing around inside my cerebellum like one of those automatic tennis ball return machines gone wild: expand my school to go all the way through high school, and call Juan Carlos, who was going to balk at the quantity of transactions I was setting up, and fly up to Miami to tell David and Candace about the latest developments in person because I wanted to see their faces glow at the news, and calculate the bank fees Juan Carlos would enjoy *before* I called him so I could hit him with the profit and cut his protestations off at the knees, and offer Charlotte a remarkable, totally non-refusable salary so she'd move down here and take charge of the academic program for the Mayan kids, and buy my own plane, holy fuck, because my business would now require frequent trips between Mérida and Miami, and I would soon be able to afford it, and get Jack fired up about the project of acquiring more banks, and fast, and fire that fat fuck, Abe, or would it be more fun to keep him around for a few more years and buy him and sell him as I saw fit because I would soon be able to afford to do that, too, and create a spreadsheet to keep track of the armored car pick-ups and deliveries because in the four days it would take one car to make a round-trip to Culiacan I could have two back from Veracruz or Oaxaca...

The truth was I didn't actually want to turn off my brain. I was enjoying the buzz.

I saw that the door of my room was ajar as I walked toward it, down the hall—the maid had once again been in to tidy up after me. I laughed as I thought about asking Pedro to be so fastidious. He was an excellent cook, and I couldn't ask for more crisply ironed clothing to be hung in my closets, and he absolutely loved spending an hour fishing the merest specks out of my pool with the long-handled net, but his attention to the mundane chores of dusting and making the bed left a lot to be desired. It occurred to me, however, that I would shortly be able to afford a housekeeper to come in a few days a week to help him out.

And then it occurred to me that in a few days, if plans moved as I certainly expected them to, I could hire a goddamn staff to come in and tend to my home in as silent and efficient a manner as Pablo's tended to his.

It was yet another heady thought, and one that straightaway started a whole new bucket of balls bouncing around my gray matter—did I *want* a goddamn staff? Pedro and I did pretty well on our own, and I could live with a little dust if it meant I didn't have to give up my privacy to maids sulking around behind me to wash up every time I took a drink of water.

"Lord," I said out loud, as I entered my room, ready to crash for an hour or so on my freshly made bed, "let me always be plagued by such rich men's problems," and drew up short, almost skidding in my retreat, when I found someone else already in it.

Alvaro.

Only his black curls were visible above the duvet that covered him, but I knew immediately it was him, and a shock of adrenaline hit me. What the *fuck* was he doing in my room? Had Pablo's man dumped him in the wrong room after Mateo knocked him silly? No—no, I'd been back to my room since then. Had he woken up, groggy, and wandered in here, lost and confused, and simply flopped on the nearest bed? That could have happened, though more than likely he had woken up, still royally pissed off, and made his way here to confront me. But then passed out again before I arrived.

Or maybe he had come to finish what Javier hadn't quite pulled off.

All of these fully formed thoughts went through my fevered brain in three seconds flat. "Hey. Asshole," I said, flipping back the duvet, figuring that if he and I were going to have it out it might as well be now as later. He was laying on his stomach and I swatted him on the back of his head. "Wake the fuck up!"

That was when I noticed all the blood.

I had always heard that head wounds bled a lot, but this was ridiculous.

"You stupid fuck," I told him, "you're bleeding all over my bed!"

I shoved his shoulder, to flip him on his back, and was momentarily bewildered when his torso turned but his head didn't.

"Oh, fuck. Oh, oh, fuck, oh, fuck, oh, *fuck*."

That was when I noticed his head wasn't actually attached to his body.

45

THE DAILY RAIN storm marched toward us like the thundering of drums—a long, ominous silence, then a crescendo that shook the tiny beach shack where the dealers were enjoying what were reputedly the best fish tacos in all of Mexico— and rocked the car where Pablo and I were huddled in the backseat. It would be a while before the weather would allow any of us to drive off to Mérida, and I certainly had no appetite.

"I think you are more upset at discovering a body than that the body you discovered was Alvaro's," Pablo said.

I thought about it. I'd been blessedly lucky all my life, to this point; the only time I'd seen death face-to-face had been in the rose-scented room of a funeral home, after the funeral director had done his work and the stark fact of death had been tempered with embalming fluid and a heavy layer of make-up. My mother *had* looked good that day—very much like herself, and at peace.

On the other hand, it really didn't matter whose body it was when you found a dead one in your bed, did it? I was crushed. Flattened and numb and, yes, my eyes were moist, but that was more a physiological reaction to shock; I certainly wasn't shedding tears over the beautiful, foolish man who'd tried to kill *me*.

"So," I asked Pablo, "what happens now?"

"How do you mean?"

"Alvaro?"

"Ah!" he sighed, as if I could possibly have had anything else on my mind. "Tonight my men will take him back to Mérida, to a funeral home there. They will give the funeral director some cash, so the widow will not be burdened, and the funeral director will not ask my men their names." He shrugged. "He will know who Alvaro is, of course. And he will then tell the wife."

I nodded. "All pretty standard," I sneered.

"'Standard' implies a *regularity* to the event," Pablo said, smooth as ever, "and I assure you what has happened is not regular operating procedure."

I took what comfort I could from his declaration. There were rules in the new world I'd entered into; Alvaro apparently hadn't followed them, and I didn't know what they were. The realization of how deeply I was in over my head caused a jolt of fear so severe it made me lurch forward. For the first time in my life the sensation of fright wasn't pleasant.

"Pablo?"

"My friend?"

I closed my eyes, and whispered. "Did you do this?"

When he didn't answer immediately, I amended my question.

"Did you have this done?"

I felt his head shake before I heard him say, "No. No, Clint, this was not me."

There was no logical reason to believe him but I did. Completely. The rain was coming down harder now. Pablo pulled a starched white cotton handkerchief from his breast pocket and leaned forward to wipe a bit of errant mud off the side of his navy blue Ferragamo's. If Pablo had ordered Alvaro's assassination, there would have been no bloody mess left on expensive sheets, or soaking through a costly feather bed.

"Then, Pablo, who *did* do it?"

Pablo sighed again, folded the handkerchief carefully, so the mud stain was on the inside, and stuffed the cloth into this coat pocket. "Well," he said slowly, "Alvaro was found in your bed." He paused in order to even more carefully measure his words. "So

I believe whoever did this, did it to show you what will happen when you cannot be trust-ed."

We sat in silence for a long while after Pablo spoke, listening to the rain fall harder on the roof of the car. Even with the storm it was a hot day, thoroughly tropical, and I be-gan to shiver with the wet under my thin suit jacket. Pablo sat serenely, his hands folded in his lap, only nodding as if in approval as the rain began to let up. Eventually I noticed the dealers begin to come out of the beach shack. They were well-fed, sated with local beer, laughing as they shook out umbrellas and opened them up, making their way back to the waiting cars.

"You know, Clint, that I must ask you this."

I waited for whatever was coming.

"Have you lost your nerve?"

I turned my head to look at him for the first time in what must have been half an hour. "Have I what?"

"The transfers. Are you still going to take care of our money, or have you lost your taste for our business? If you have, you must tell me, and then I will tell you all the reasons why you should not do that."

46

Amongst his many skills and in spite of his shortcomings, Pedro had always been attuned to my moods—though I was not a terribly moody person so I suppose this wasn't an exceptional talent. Nevertheless, he noticed my sober demeanor and mirrored it, thoughtfully welcoming me home and removing himself to unpack for me and start on my laundry.

"Would you like something to drink," he asked before he disappeared into the bedroom. "A... a cup of tea?"

"When have you ever known me to drink tea?" I asked, and smiled at him. He was right, however, that I needed some sort of comfort, and it took me a good fifteen minutes of sitting on a lounge chair by my pool, brooding, to figure out what it was. "I'm going out for a while," I called down the hall to him. He didn't answer, and I wasn't sure he'd heard me, but I pocketed my keys and headed out the door.

I tried to call Jack as I drove—I hadn't figured out what to say to him, but he was going to have to know Alvaro was dead sooner or later; he was going to have to help me deal with Alvaro's account at the bank. My call went straight to voice mail so I left a message for him to call me back and told Siri to dial Juan Carlos.

"Eight million *a day*," Juan Carlos said by way of greeting.

"Starting day after tomorrow," I replied.

"You don't give a person a lot of notice—"

"Eighty thousand a day in fees, Juan Carlos. Your promotion is all but carved in stone—it wouldn't surprise me if you were named president in short order. So, no, not a lot of notice, but that's not required when you're bringing as much to the party as I am."

We hung up just as I pulled into the curb in front of my school. It was late in the evening and the workers had gone home for the day, so I dug my keys out of my pocket and let myself in.

The project was in better condition than I'd thought it would be. New concrete floors had been poured throughout, and imbedded with different, traditional ceramic tile patterns in each room. Miguel had also fabricated wall sconces for the corners of each room, and the eighteen-foot ceilings were finished off with a six-inch crown molding. The fountain I'd commissioned him to create, big as a swimming pool, was nearly complete; a life-sized statue of the Mayan god, Coyopa, god of thunder, had been fixed in the center. When the plumbing was installed, water would flow from his mouth.

My tour of the buildings included the small office on the first floor that Miguel and I were sharing for the duration of the construction. It held a desk, a couple of chairs, a bookcase where Miguel stashed his plans and drawings and a few odd tools. The desk held a lamp, the phone that was connected to the landline I'd installed for the school, and a legal pad where Miguel left messages for me to pick up if he wasn't there when I came by. Two more sets of parents had stopped by inquiring about enrolling their sons, bringing the student roster to thirty-four. I didn't even have a name yet for the place and we were almost halfway to full student capacity. I thought again of Charlotte, how much I wanted her here with me in Mérida, and for how many different reasons; she and the kids would love each other. The mayor of the city had also come by to thank me personally for helping out with the city's youth, giving them a chance to improve themselves. Without my school these kids would never have been able to afford to attend a private school, much less a language school, and I was pleased with this show of support from the local government.

The desk also held a framed photograph of my beloved Taavi, his beautiful, brown eyes still shining with life. I couldn't yet bear any reminder of him in the home I had hoped to share with him but, here, at the school I was creating in his honor, it would have been inappropriate for him not to have a presence.

I had come to Mérida on what was supposed to have been a two-week vacation. I'd always enjoyed traveling; I had recently been freed from the jail sentence I'd received for running an escort service, and I had the funds available to go wherever it was I wanted to go, and I had chosen the Yucatan in which to begin what I assumed at the time would rather be a world tour. I had been traveling alone—the only person I'd have wanted along for my adventures was Jack and he'd been unable to get away—so, on the second night of my stay in Mérida, looking for a little companionship, I'd gone out to a gay bar. Amongst the Spanish and Mayans in linen shorts and guayaberas, I stood out like a DEA agent with my blonde hair and Brooks Brothers' gear. Several men approached me as I stood at the bar, trying to order a drink. Taavi had been among them. He was a small man, as Mayans tend to be, but he looked directly into my eyes as he asked me to dance with all the assurance of the young god he could have passed for.

We hadn't left each other's sides for the rest of the evening, and ended up spending the rest of the week together at my hotel. He was disconcertingly truthful with me, right from the start, as most people I'd ever known would never have been. He'd told of the struggles his people faced in their own country. Of how he had strived to learn English. How that accomplishment had led to a menial job on a construction crew. How his diligence to the job and knack for the work had led to an arc of promotions—including being a regular part of crews building an arch bridge in Louisiana and a truss bridge in Ohio, and, finally, a scholarship to the University of Southern Indiana, which has a robust international program, to study engineering. He inspired a sort of honesty from me that, at first, felt unnatural. But I told him everything, and he listened without judgment, only teasing me for how materialistic he thought I was.

At the end of the week, he'd taken me to meet his family where they still lived in their ancestral village a few miles outside of Méri-da—his parents, his grandmother, his broth-er and sister, five people who lived together in a pristinely clean but exceptionally tiny home, about six hundred square feet, by my calculations. "Taavi", they told me, meant "adored", and that this was true was without question. Taavi's relatives were proud of all of his accomplishments, but it was a pride without price—I understood that even with-out his engineering degree, their love and admiration for him would be unchanged, still enormous and complete. They were the happiest people I'd ever met in my life. I couldn't believe my luck—that Taavi and his family were inviting me to share such a life. Such simple, complete contentment.

And then, one day a little over six months before, when the renovations for the home Taavi and I would share were well underway, and we were in the midst of a running ar-gument with his family over my insistence that they all come to live with us for at least a part of each year, while Taavi was away supervising the construction of a pony truss bridge in Kentucky, I got the phone call that told me he was gone. He'd lost his footing while conducting a routine inspection and plunged into Big Bracken Creek. The creek was no deep, roiling waterway, but Taavi had hit his head on a rock upon landing, and he was gone before any of his co-workers could climb down to the waterline and offer help.

I took one more, long glance at Taavi's photo and turned it over on my desk before tears could come. I opened the bottom left corner of the desk and pulled out the bottle of Jameson's I kept there. Nothing like good, old Irish whiskey as a companion for the evenings I spent at this desk with Taavi, sketching out plans for what I privately thought of as *his* school or pouring over the financials; it would serve as well now for comfort. I held it up to the lamp and was surprised to see it still so full since I knew Miguel knew all about the stash. I picked up the old Starbucks cup I kept with the bottle in the drawer and poured a long shot.

I leaned against the desktop while I drank and tried to put my finger on the core of my discontent. I kept coming back to a feeling of being let down and laughed at myself; nothing like death and murder to take the joy out of something. "Well, fool," I said to the walls of that small room, "you'd better get over yourself—you have one day to ramp up and launch a business for people you really, really don't want to fuck over."

I downed the rest of my Scotch and was about to lock up and head out when my cell rang—Xavier calling. I held the phone in my hand for a few rings, deciding whether or not to answer. Xavier had been texting me frequently since we'd renewed our friendship. I could easily figure out what he wanted—to renew more than simple friendship—and I wasn't sure I wanted to do that. I couldn't deny that my attraction to him hadn't waned much at all in the intervening years, but he had been a controlling friend. I was older now, and wiser, and his domineering ways would no longer fly—and I very seriously doubted that Xavier would have changed a whole lot, so what was the point?

Besides, there was Charlotte now to think about.

Except that he was calling now, actually reaching out voice-to-voice instead of only texting and that intrigued me. I would probably spend the rest of my life wondering why I answered.

"Hey, Xavier."

"Hi, Clint. Glad you picked up. What have you been up to?"

I got lightheaded with the impossibility of giving him an honest answer and I plopped down behind the desk. "Not much. You?"

I heard a sigh on the other end of the line that sounded far too like anguish for my comfort. "Clint, I'm calling as legal counsel for Citizen's National Bank."

That got my skin prickling.

"Clint, I don't know how to tell you this,

so I'll tell it as I've heard it."

I swallowed. "Sounds like a plan."

"Jack had lunch with Sharon today— Abe's wife?"

"Yeah, I knew about that."

"Abe told her he wants a divorce."

I laughed. "Abe told Sharon? Not the other way around?"

"No, not the other way around, Clint. He left her and, in response, she told Jack something—"

"Jack mentioned she'd said she had something over on him." I laughed again. "What was it?"

"He was embezzling from the bank, Clint."

I didn't know whether to cry or shit. "Holy fuck, Xavier. Is it true?"

Now it was his turn to swallow. "I've spent all afternoon with David looking at the documents and, yes. It does seem to be true."

"How much."

"Two million. Minimum. Jack's already contacted the Feds and they're going to arrest Abe tomorrow."

"Not tonight? He'll run—what's stopping him from running?"

"Abe doesn't know we know, and he won't until the Feds show up and take him away tomorrow."

My poor, overworked brain. I was ecstatic that Abe had been caught red-handed. Baffled that David had apparently lost upwards of two million and hadn't noticed. Blindsided that a stupid fuck like Abe could have been smart enough to run such an expensive scam right under his father's nose—and might have gotten away with it if he hadn't pulled the idiotic move of telling his wife he was leaving before he made his getaway. Wretched for David, and Candace, and Jack, at Abe's betrayal. Pissed because I was now a primary shareholder of Citizen's National Bank and it was me Abe had stolen from.

"I'll want to see those documents, Xavier."

"Of course."

"I'll ask Jack to send you my e-mail address—you should have it in any case. How are Candace and David?"

There was a pause while Xavier thought. "Candace is strong. She's the one who insisted we not do anything to interfere with the plans for Abe's arrest, let him be jolted like that, she says. Then she wants me to find an attorney to represent him, which she says she and David will pay for personally. David? He's aged twenty years in the last few hours."

I yanked my bottle of Scotch out of the bottom desk drawer, poured myself another healthy shot and threw it back.

"There's one more thing, Clint."

"Of course there is." I refilled my Starbucks mug.

"Abe had a partner... An accomplice."

"Well, that explains a lot—I knew he was too stupid to pull something like this on his own."

"A woman, and Jack says you know her."

I froze, the mug at my lips, waiting for Xavier to continue.

"Abe's secretary, Clint. A woman named Charlotte Cruet."

My heart fell, and so did the arm that was holding the mug. The Jameson's spilled all over my lap. "Fuck," I said.

"Are you all right, Clint?"

"Yes," I said quickly, mopping at my pants with some of Miguel's sketches. "Yes, I am, and not that I'm not happy you called Xavier, but now I know why Jack didn't call me and tell me all this himself."

47

PABLO WAS GRACIOUS, as always, when I called and asked him if I could use his plane. "I'll tell my people to have it ready for you within the hour," he said.

"Sooner, if possible, Pablo. Please."

I locked up the school and drove directly to the airport. I'd grabbed one of the yellow legal pads Miguel used to make his sketches and a couple of his pencil stubs from the office and used my time in the air to create the transport grid, according to the dealer's lottery numbers—and I was abjectly grateful to have such a tedious task to occupy my mind for the two-hour flight.

I arrived in Miami after ten and worked my way through the airport, bustling even at that hour with tourists either disappointed their holiday was over or eager for it to start: bikini babes and bros, women whose leathery, sun-baked skin made them look twice as old as they were and women whose facelifts made them look like ageless aliens, grandmas with chipped pink nail polish, and men just this side of being too decrepit to play another round of golf. People who thought Miami was paradise didn't have a clue; it was a zoo. I stepped around a young girl wearing a pair of Daisy Dukes with cowboy boots and what I thought were lace stockings until I realized her legs were just covered with massive, intricate tattoos, all the while I had both hands on my phone typing "Charlotte Cruet, Homestead, Florida" into my browser.

I could find no address for a Charlotte Cruet but there was one for a Chester that looked promising, and that was where I directed my cab driver. It was a neighborhood near where my grandparents had once lived, now a Cuban enclave. I walked up the two concrete steps to the bungalow's front door and knocked quickly, before I could ask myself one more time, *What the fuck are you doing here*, and come up with an answer that might deter me.

Charlotte answered the door. For all my frantic, focused efforts to get to this door, I didn't once expect finding her to be this easy. She was wearing a yellow chenille bathrobe pulled tightly around her waist, her hair pulled back off her lovely forehead in a ponytail. Her father, Chester, weathered and brown, wore a much duller green plaid number and peeked around her to see who was at the door.

"Mr. Clint! Charlotte, this is David and Candace's friend, you met him at their house, I think."

"I did," Charlotte said. She smiled even as she asked, "What are you doing here... at this hour of the night?"

"Mr. Cruet, I never thanked you properly for the beautiful cape you gave to my friend. He liked it so very much, and, he asks... he asks me to send his thanks as well."

"Oh." Chester nodded, no less puzzled than I was about what I *was* doing there. "It was my pleasure."

"Well, we really do, both, thank you."

It was only then that Chester invited me in, and Charlotte stepped aside to allow me to enter. We stood in the narrow hallway too long, until I said, "You know, I know it's late, and I could really use a cup of coffee."

"Oh, of course," Charlotte said.

"I'll help you." I quickly took her arm and let it look as if she was leading me into their kitchen. "You don't mind, do you, Chester? We'll be right back with coffee..."

"What in heaven's name," Charlotte said as I hustled her through the swinging dining room door and toward the coffeemaker on the counter.

"I..." I had no idea where to start. I couldn't even look at her for fear her angel face would distract me. "I'm not here to judge. We all do the things we need to do to survive, Charlotte."

She tilted her head and the motion caught me off guard. I glanced up at her. She was looking at me as if she knew some of the things I'd done to survive.

I looked away and bulldozed on. "But I know what you and Abe have done."

This got the reaction I dreaded; Charlotte gasped and put a hand to her mouth. I had not wanted proof of her guilt and now I had it.

"I don't care why you did it—maybe you felt they owed it to you, for all the years your father worked for them, or the way Jack and I treated you when we were kids, or... I don't know and I don't care. But I do know what you did, and David and Candace know, and Jack knows, and their lawyer knows. And the Feds know."

Charlotte sank into one of the kelly green, vinyl-covered chairs at the table.

"What's going to happen now?" she whispered.

"Well, Abe's going to be arrested tomorrow."

She nodded. "And me?"

"You too," I said, and tears sprang to her eyes. "Unless you do the smart thing right now."

"What's that?"

I sat down beside her at the table. "Come with me to see my friend, Xavier. He's an attorney for the bank. Tell him what you know, provide evidence about how you and Abe embezzled the money, tell them where the money is so they can recover it. You'll probably still get probation, but you won't go to jail."

Charlotte sat back, and her eyes narrowed. "Suppose I don't do that. Suppose I just go get Abe right now and we leave. Right now. Just slip out of town and nobody—"

"Then you spend a couple of days, maybe a week, running from the Feds and, when they find you—which, they *will* find you, Charlotte—you're definitely in jail." I pushed the table away from me. "Come on, Charlotte! Yeah, Abe might run away with you tonight, because he's stupid enough to do that, but when you get caught, do you really think he's going to give a shit about what happens to you? He's going to do whatever he has to do to keep his own fat ass out of jail. You know he's going to do that! And, you know what, people are going to believe him when he tells them you're the brains behind the embezzlement because, God knows, even his own parents know he's too much of a moron to have pulled this off on his own. So why don't you do what you have to do for yourself, before he gets a chance to turn on you?"

Charlotte sat, stock still, for several minutes. Then she looked at me and said, "Let me get dressed."

48

XAVIER AND I sat in his BMW, down the street from the main office of Citizen's National but with a clear view of the front door. I watched the digital clock on his dashboard. At 9:01 we'd watched as David walked into the building, followed by Jack at 9:10, and Abe at 9:13. It was now 9:25.

"He's going to get suspicious that Charlotte's not in the office yet."

Xavier shook his head. "So his secretary's a little late. The Feds will be here before he starts to wonder about it."

"She wasn't just his secretary. As we both know."

Xavier took a careful sip from his paper cup of take-out coffee. "You took an awful chance last night, Clint."

I couldn't disagree, so I said nothing.

"*Why?*"

"Xavier, if you're looking for a rock-solid rationale, you're not going to get it from me. All I care about is that Charlotte isn't going to be led out of that building in handcuffs in a few minutes."

"You prefer that she's sitting pretty, probably at her father's kitchen table drinking her morning coffee right now, likely to get off scot-free for robbing you of two million dollars?"

I took a sip of my own coffee in response.

Xavier elbowed me. "There goes David."

I looked up to see David exiting the bank's main entrance, standing and chatting with a security guard, his right hand in his front pant pocket, jiggling his keys. That nervous gesture, so customary, nearly killed me. I was silently grateful when the valet brought his car around from the garage, and David got behind the wheel and drove away. It had been arranged with the Feds: David needed to show up at the office in the morning, in order that Abe wasn't tipped off that this wasn't going to be just another ordinary day, but he could leave the premises before the actual arrest. He didn't want to see it, and no one was going to make him. He was heading home to gather up Candace to make the eleven-fifteen flight for Freeport, an open-ended trip to the Bahamas. Jack would call them and keep them informed, and he and Candace would decide when they should return, once the circus had left town.

"I worry about them," I said. "David and Candace."

Xavier shrugged. "They never had any illusions about their sons. In fact, I think they're pretty amazed that Jack's stepped up to the plate the way he has during all of this."

"Yeah." I agreed; I was proud of Jack, too. "Hey, here's what I don't understand—Sharon's the one who tipped Jack off to all of this, but she's being named as a co-defendant?"

"That's the rich part. Apparently she'd known about the scheme for a few years and she was fine with it. She was even fine with the girlfriend because, you know, she was living pretty high because of all the money coming in, and Abe promised her a hundred thousand dollars, tax-free and clear, if she ever wanted to leave him. Turns out Abe really just wanted her to be the one to leave the marriage and thought a hundred thousand bucks would do it. Sharon, though, found out how much money was actually involved, and she wanted half of it—one clean million—which Abe was not prepared to part with. So she ratted him out." Xavier chuckled. "She surely didn't think that move through." He drank some more coffee.

"Greed, Clint," he said, "gets everybody in the end."

Xavier and I sat in silence for a minute, and then we saw three long, black SUVs pull in front of the bank, park in the No Parking zone right at the main entrance. The front doors of the cars opened simultaneously, driver and passenger sides, as if choreographed, and a dark-suited man stepped out of each door and headed for the bank's doors. The security guards stepped aside and let them pass.

It was a matter of only minutes then— three or four at most—before the first news van pulled up, and a reporter raced out and up to one of the guards to start asking her questions, followed by a harried cameraman trying to keep a steady hand.

"Who do you think tipped off the press?" I asked as another, and then another news van skidded onto the street, one of them discharging its eager journalist even before it had come to a complete stop.

"I have no idea," Xavier said, "but here we go."

49

ARRIVED BACK IN Mérida later that afternoon. My first armored truck was due from Villahermosa, Tomas's territory, the following morning. Juan Carlos had already hired one extra body, in consideration of the volume we were going to be running through his bank, and an additional computer terminal was being installed even as I drove my car back from the airport.

Jack had decided, with all the attention Abe's arrest had drawn to the bank, to spread the dormant accounts around, involve more customers who'd opened their accounts at branch offices, and he'd moved the base of operations—the terminals at which the wires would be received—to their office in Boynton Beach. He'd already hired the friend I'd recommended, Jocelyn, to remake the bank's loan department, and was accepting résumés to fill a position he'd created, Vice President of Acquisitions—his feeling being that the more failing banks we absorbed, and the more dormant accounts we had access to, the less exposure we would have. I agreed and he was moving on it.

As I turned on to the Paseo de Montao, I realized I was about to embark on a path I hadn't traveled in years: having a nine-to-five, five-day-a-week job. I'd focused almost exclusively on remuneration and it was just hitting me what I'd signed up for, in terms of a grueling schedule. Not that the time commitment bothered me—not in the least; as David would say, I was a lucky man because I wasn't lazy. Still, there were tasks that would need to be dealt with in order to keep my new enterprise running smoothly and they would be hard to accomplish sitting in Juan Carlos's office for eight hours every weekday. What I needed was an assistant, I thought, and the next thought I had was *Tim*. Alvaro's steward. I had no idea what his qualifications might be, beyond being excellent at taking orders, but that was a primary virtue as far as I was concerned. I wasn't even sure what his last name was, but I knew I could track him down if I wanted to.

I suppose I shouldn't have been surprised that the old, well-guarded entry at Alvaro's hacienda was abandoned. His thugs had moved on quickly to find employment elsewhere. I slowed to five miles an hour, creeping toward the house. I wasn't even sure Alvaro's wife would be home, but as I neared the house I could hear the screams of children in conflict. Alvaro, Junior and Javi were definitely in.

"Sofia?"

I found her sitting on a sofa in the dark living room off the courtyard. She was wearing a sundress and drinking a glass of wine, the children still heard but not seen.

"Do you remember me? I was a friend of Alvaro's—"

She turned her head toward me when I spoke. "Clint," she said.

"Yes."

She ran a hand through her dark, unkempt hair. "It's nice of you to come. Not many people around here now. Not since I have nothing left to give them." She spoke as if Alvaro had been dead for years and years. "My mother is coming later. And Oscar. Alvaro's brother. Did you know he had a brother? He would never see Alvaro, all those years, because he says Alvaro is a criminal. But today he calls me and tells me he is coming here. I think he wants me to be grateful to him for it." She held her glass toward me. "Would you like a glass too?"

"Um, no. Thank you."

She shrugged and took a drink.

"Sofia, I'm here to help you." I reached into my breast pocket and withdrew the copy of the latest statement from Alvaro's account at Citizen's National that Jack had supplied. "Before Alvaro died, I helped him open this bank account. He told me, if anything happened to him, I was to make sure to give it to you. So"—I placed the statement on the table between us—"here."

Sofia looked at me, and at the statement, then sat up slowly and picked it up. She seemed disinterested as she unfolded it, looking it over with a more experienced eye than I might have imagined, quickly finding the balance, which made her eyes grow wide.

"This is mine?"

"It is," I confirmed.

"Dios mio!" she cried. "All mine?"

I nodded. "All sixteen million of it. You have more money than you will ever need, and I'm willing to help you make even more of it. The real estate market in the U.S. is a great buying opportunity now. Don't you worry about it today, we can talk about all of that later."

"Dios mio!" She laughed and launched herself into my lap, holding my face between her hands and covering it with kisses. The old me would have regretted that I hadn't kept some of that money for myself—after all, she hadn't even known the account existed. The new me wanted to give her sixteen million dollars, and more. I liked the feeling. And Taavi would have approved.

As I drove away, headed back to my house, my cell rang.

"Hello, Pablo," I said when I answered. "We're all set to start work bright and early tomorrow morning."

"Good!" he said. "Good man!"

For the first time, possibly in my life, I believed that I would have at least half a chance if the topic were ever truly up for debate.

Pablo and I chatted for a few minutes— he wanted me to provide a copy of the transport grid I'd created to the men in his control room in Chuburna; he believed they could track the money deliveries more efficiently with their technology than I could on paper and I said that I agreed with him.

"Good! Good!" I could hear Pablo's smile over the phone.

"Anything else, Pablo?"

"No, no, I think that is all that was on my mind."

"OK, then," I told him. I pressed a button to roll down my driver's side window, the breeze brisk and refreshing, while I waited for him to hang up. When he had, I grinned down at my phone. I was the child of a single, working mother and, even given the status I had attained in the world, I deplored waste. It seemed a shame to trash a perfectly functional cell phone, and the idea chafed against the values of "waste not, want not" my mother had so lovingly instilled in me.

Still, I'd bought the phone nearly a year before. It had to be time for an upgrade in any case, I thought, and tossed it out the window. I watched it bump along the asphalt behind me for a few seconds, and then I lifted my head to enjoy the chill air around my face as I drove.

MONEY FAUCET and *HARD CASH*, the second and third installments of the Clint Kennedy Series coming soon from Joe Calderwood. Sign up for our newsletter and be the first to know when they're released.

https://mailchi.mp/waterstreetpressbooks.com/waterstreetcrimemailinglist

Get the Water Street Crime Starter Library
FOR FREE

Get four, full-length ebooks—the thrillers **BLOODY PARADISE, FROM ICE TO ASHES, TROPICAL ICE**, and **SING FOR THE DEAD**—plus two introductory short stories by the author of **STAINED FORTUNE** and lots more exclusive content, all for free.

Building a relationship with our readers is the very best thing about publishing. We occasionally send newsletters with details on new releases, special offers and other bits of news relating to Water Street Press.

And if you sign up to the mailing list we'll send you all this free stuff:

1. A free ebook edition of the exotic thriller **BLOODY PARADISE**—"...a spicy thriller..."

2. A free ebook edition of the crime thriller **FROM ICE TO ASHES**—"designed to shoot the ice down your spine..."

3. A free ebook edition of the eco-thriller **TROPICAL ICE**—"...well-spun, tautly written..."

4. A free ebook edition of the delightfully noir-ish mystery **SING FOR THE DEAD**—Foreword Reviews' Gold Medal winner

5. A free copy of two introductory short stores from the author of **STAINED FORTUNE**—stories from the childhoods of two of his most intriguing characters, Alvaro and Pablo.

6. Advance notice about the release of the next two novels in the Clint Kennedy Series, ***MONEY FAUCET*** and ***HARD CASH***.

You can get all this and more,
for free, just by signing up at

**https://mailchi.mp/waterstreetpressbooks/
clintkennedy**

Did you enjoy this book? You can make a big difference for our amazing Water Street Crime authors.

Reviews are the most powerful tools in our arsenal when it comes getting attention for our books. Much as we'd like to, we don't have the financial muscle of a New York publisher. We can't take out full-page ads in the newspaper or put posters on the subway.

(Not yet, anyway).

But we do have something much more powerful and effective than that, and it's something that those publishers would kill to get their hands on.

A committed and loyal bunch of readers.

Honest reviews of our books help bring them to the attention of other readers.

If you've enjoyed this book we would be very grateful if you could spend just five minutes on Amazon or the online vendor of your choice leaving a review (it can be as short as you like).

Here's the link to Amazon, if that's your preferred vendor: **https://amzn.to/2Zo0R55**

Thank you very much.

ABOUT THE AUTHOR

JOE CALDERWOOD WAS born and raised in Homestead, Florida and graduated from college in 1971 with a BBA. For many years he was a practicing CPA in Florida before beginning his career as a serial entrepreneur. He's owned, so far, seven different businesses, currently a fifty-five lot development in Western North Carolina. *Stained Fortune* is his first novel, and the first in the planned three-part Clint Kennedy series. He lives in Western North Carolina with his spouse of three years—though the two have lived together thirty-six years, only recently the Supreme Court allowed them to marry.

ALSO FROM WATER STREET PRESS

Ready for more thrills?

We suggest **The Grand**, by Dennis D. Wilson, the first in his Dean Wister Crime Series.

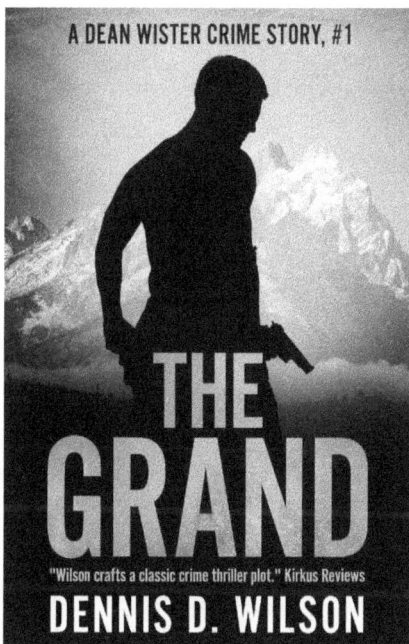

Have you read all the books in the Water Street Crime collection? Check out Water Street Press at this link and see all the amazing books we have to offer:

https://www.waterstreetpressbooks.com

1

SATURDAY, OCTOBER 31, 2009

Halloween. All Hallow's fucking Eve. I stood in the office of a dead lawyer. Adrenaline, long my drug of choice, pumped through my body like a mariachi band playing in my brain. The body slumped in the cheap, cocoa-brown, vinyl-covered office chair behind the badly battered, olive-green metal desk, and the head—what was left of it; what wasn't spattered on the fake oak paneling behind the ugly desk—was thrown back against the headrest, his eyes wide open, frozen in shock at his own demise. A jointed paper skeleton hung over the window on the far side of the office and danced in the breeze from the air conditioning unit directly beneath it—an homage to the season contributed, no doubt, by the attorney's secretary, a dowdy woman I'd found strange and irritating on the one occasion we'd met. Someone had replaced a broken pane in the window with cardboard and duct tape, probably... What was her name? Carla?

The lamp on the dead man's desk burned dimly, throwing patches of eerie light over the blood spatters on his argyle-patterned polo shirt, the lap of his khaki pants, the unopened McDonald's paper bag that sat before him on the desk. One of his legs—the one he limped on—was propped by the heel on the top of an upturned waste can. The details hit me like a series of photographs—click, click, click—and each image burned into my brain. I would never again believe a witness to a crime who says he didn't see anything.

I panted fiercely, as if I'd just run a hard ten miles in ninety-degree heat. And the sweat—instantaneous and profuse. I could smell myself, the scent of exertion. Or was it the stink of fear? I suddenly understood why some people piss themselves when they panic, though I had not yet descended that far into distress.

"Shit, shit, shit!" I didn't know what to do. My instinct was to call the police, but the dead lawyer was an adversary of mine at the time of his demise—I had plenty of reasons to want him dead and I didn't know if the cops would buy my story: *This is the way I found him when I walked in.* Which was true.

"Coulter!" I'd shouted as I'd walked in through his office door. The front office had been empty, as I'd expected it to be at that hour of the night, so I'd shouted again. "Coulter! Answer me! Where the hell are you?"

Jessie Coulter had acquiesced to my insistence that he and I, surely two reasonable men, could broker an agreement to settle our dispute without having to drag it through the court; he'd agreed to meet with me one last time. Alone. At his office. At ten o'clock at night. When everyone else in the entire shoddy strip mall where his practice was located would be gone for the day. But the timing was my fault; I'd insisted he meet me today, before I flew back home to Mérida after what had turned out to be a week's involuntary vacation in Miami, but I wouldn't cut short my Halloween celebration with the Cohens to accommodate him a few hours earlier. I was being perverse, making this shady ambulance chaser meet me on my terms. I cared deeply about the Cohen's, of course, but I didn't give a flying fuck about the holiday, and even less about seeing their grandchildren—Abe's dubious spawn—dressed up in the Harry Potter and Hermoine Granger costumes Candace had whipped up on short notice. Why did I have to be so goddamn contrary all the time? Look where it had gotten me.

I knew next to nothing about crime detection, even less about forensics, only what I'd seen on the police procedurals I sometimes caught on TV. It didn't cross my mind that no matter how suspicious the police might be of me, my innocence would, of course, be proved eventually because the lawyer would have died at an earlier hour, one for which I had an air-tight alibi—I'd been with either Jack or Xavier all day, and at the Cohens', where drink service began at five PM sharp, since the cocktail hour had started. Also, there was no murder weapon in the room to which I could be linked— Wait... I moved my eyes to scan all the surfaces in the room— the dented desk, the bare, crusty floor, the rusted file cabinets, the credenza which was spattered with too much gray matter for my taste. Strangely, in the corners and along the baseboards and all among the stacks of over-stuffed file folders spread out on the floor, there was a collection of brightly colored, lint-covered jelly beans. But, no, there was no gun anywhere that I could see.

And what would I do with a gun if I found

one? I had no idea. In my panic, I would probably have picked the fucking thing up and got my fingerprints all over it.

Glad there was no gun, then. Just a dead lawyer who had—gun or no gun—clearly been shot quite expertly, smack between the eyes.

Other than at funerals, at which a dead body is seen in only the most sanitized state, I'd seen only one other dead body before in my entire life. The memory of *that* murder— of finding Alvaro lifeless in my bed deep in Pablo's luxurious underground bunker— crept like a thick fog into my brain. I shook my head to clear it and drew in a long breath. The air in the small, closed office had the metallic tang of blood and French fry grease and I gagged. Then I slapped myself. Hard. "Pull yourself together, man. *Focus.*"

At the heart of my dilemma was not a concern about eventual exoneration for the crime before me; unless someone was trying to frame me, exoneration was a certainty. What I was worried about was the police getting all up in my business while they were figuring out I had nothing to do with the lawyer's death. That I couldn't have had anything to do with it. I had to do something—but—

What? Something more proactive than standing dumbfounded and gagging in an office with a dead bargain-basement attorney until someone—a wife? a client? that annoying secretary?—missed the slob and came looking to find out what had happened to him.

I suddenly heard a cell phone start to ring. I knew it wasn't my phone—no self-respecting criminal would be cheesy enough to use the theme from *The Sopranos* as his ring tone. But hearing the familiar tune sent another wave of adrenaline coursing through my veins. "Shit, shit, *shit!*"